Couples by Intention

Creating and Cultivating Relationships that Matter

❖

Elliott Kronenfeld, Ph.D., LICSW, CSTS

Couples by Intention: Creating and Cultivating Relationships that Matter,
Published January, 2018

Editorial and proofreading services: John Harrell, Beth Raps, Karen Grennan
Interior layout: Howard Johnson
Cover Design: Dimitrios Gripeos and Howard Johnson

Photo credits: Author photo by Matt McKee
Rendered figures designed by Dimitrios Gripeos and owned by Elliott
Kronenfeld, Ph.D., LICSW, CSTS

SDP Publishing

Published by SDP Publishing, an imprint of SDP Publishing Solutions, LLC.

To obtain permission(s) to use material from this work, please submit a written request to:

SDP Publishing
Permissions Department
PO Box 26, East Bridgewater, MA 02333
or email your request to info@SDPPublishing.com.

ISBN-13 (print): 978-0-9992839-4-3
ISBN-13 (e-book): 978-0-9992839-5-0

Library of Congress Control Number: 2017960255

Here's what people are saying about "Couples by Intention"

"*Couples by Intention* is a gem! All the expertise of an experienced couple's therapist is offered in a highly readable and engaging narrative. Readers will feel like they have a wise and caring friend sitting next to them, giving them practical strategies, telling them instructive stories, all delivered with warmth and compassion. Different from other books on this topic, and more revelatory, *Couples by Intention* explores Kronenfeld's innovative couple's therapy group in great detail. The tools and strategies come to life in this group, as do the people in it. Readers will undoubtedly resonate with the couple's stories and struggles, and will benefit from witnessing their healing. This is a great resource for couples and clinicians alike."

—Miri Skolnik, Psy.D.
Assistant Dean
Student Support Services
MIT

"Elliott's group brought many gifts to us. We learned we are not alone, that other people have similar issues to us, and we found inspiration in the progress other couples made. We always left feeling motivated and uplifted. He gave us a lot of tools and language that we were able to take back to apply to our relationship as well as other relationships in our lives."

—"Blake"

Dedication

For Michael and Olivia,
the most intentional decisions
I have ever made

Table of Contents

The essential power of curiosity in relationships; how to listen actively with your partner (and show it!); the "four buckets" of emotions—and how easy it is to confuse one emotion for another.

In order to care for others, you have to put yourself first; creating "sacred space" with your partner; why it's important to draw boundaries around your relationship.

More about how assumptions can harm a relationship; what it is you want to achieve in the relationship; how to come home from work each day.

Why it's so important to have a sense of who you are (internal alignment) and to live authentically (external alignment); watching out for "timelines" that others may seek to impose on your relationship without your consent.

Living in "plateau" moments in your relationship; it's normal for couples to be working on different aspects of their relationship at varying paces all at once.

Acknowledgments

In early 2015, I was in Boca de Tomatlan, Mexico, with a talented group of sex therapists, medical practitioners, and sex educators. We had spent a week at the Casa de los Artistas sharing our experience and learning how to expand our practice of sex therapy, guided by the amazing Gina Ogden, PhD, LMFT, and Tina Nevin. At varying points in the week, my colleagues and friends asked me, "Where is the book? You have something to say, and we need to know when the book is coming out."

I hemmed and hawed until the last day, when I suddenly had an "Aha!" moment and realized that there *was* a book in me after all. So, in front of everybody, Gina asked me to name the book.

I responded with, *"The Yet-To-Be-Titled Book of Couples and Intimacy,* by Elliott Kronenfeld." Everyone laughed, and then Gina said, "No. Really. I want you to open your crown chakra and let the book fall into you. What is it called?" I responded with the title you now know, and just like that, the book was born.

I've been on this journey with several fellow travelers who have each made the adventure rich and meaningful. Without them there would be no book, no practice in Boston, nothing.

First, and with the humblest appreciation, I thank the couples who have allowed me to join them in their quest to get closer to one another. Being a witness to your growth and wisdom has changed me in untold ways. I am honored to be alongside you, and you have taught me much.

To Marty, who showed me that working through challenges can unleash ability: your insight, support, wisdom, and guidance ensured that we could cross the finish line. This is as much yours as anyone else's. And to Michael, who reminded me that when the work was challenging, sometimes a quick quip can set you right: my heartfelt thanks.

To the Tribe, because the Tribe creates your vibe, my gratitude—and especially to Amy, Llere, and Dimitri, who always answered the calls, fixed the problems, built the systems, and made me look capable.

To my editor, John, who was so insightful and talented to smooth out the bumps and fill in the potholes: you are a complete joy and gift, for which I am so very grateful.

To Lisa and the team of SDP Publishing, who was with me when this book was something else entirely all those years ago: thanks for the encouragement to just write.

Thanks to Yara and Estefania, who ensure that this Colibri flies. And to Gina, Tina, and the 4-D Network, thanks for warming me in all quadrants.

To my amazing readers: thank you for the feedback; it was perfection.

To my special care team of John and Alexis: thanks for ensuring that I was at my best.

To Tressa and Miri, who inspired me to leave my old life behind and start this work: you were right, so very right.

To Grandma Annie: thanks for reminding me to *do my work*.

To my intentional partner, Joe: I choose you. To my amazing kids, Michael and Olivia, who remind me every second of every day of the power of curiosity, and for inspiring me to want to challenge whatever messages aren't working: you are everything.

Introduction

"I don't know how it got so fucked up. I thought I was doing what I was supposed to be doing and she left me anyway! What did I do wrong?"

Chris couldn't understand why his marriage to Kelly had ended. Five years had gone by since his divorce, and he still didn't have the knowledge or words to explain why he was single and starting over again. Now that he had started a new relationship with a woman named Aileen, he was terrified that he'd find himself in the same lonely and confusing place all over again. The fear was stopping Chris from being fully present with Aileen, and he had come to my office for counseling.

Every day, countless individuals experience something like Chris's fear, as dating partners, spouses, and significant others try to figure out the do's and don'ts for healthy intimacy in real-time, wondering how in the world they're supposed to build relationships that last without having received any training as to *how*. Intimate relationships are some of the greatest challenges we willingly take on, but we aren't given classes on how to navigate relationships, how to sail the mysterious, often unpredictable waters of becoming close to the people around us.

This book is that class. *Couples by Intention* is a step-by-step, guided tour for relationships, a how-to for creating intimacy with another person. As you read these chapters, you'll be eavesdropping on the multi-week program that I facilitate at my practice near Boston for couples who are determined to grow in their love, enjoyment, and closeness with each other. The program, like this book, is called "Couples by Intention," and as you

▼

We aren't given classes on how to navigate relationships, how to sail the mysterious, often unpredictable waters of becoming close to the people around us.

▲

read through these pages and try out the exercises I've included, you'll gain some of the same insights and work on many of the same skills that my clients develop as they come to my sessions each week. If you've never been to group therapy before (which I highly recommend for couples who are eager to grow together and ready to do the work) or if it's not possible for you to do so right now, this book will give you the next-best thing. The book isn't meant to be a form of therapy or a replacement for skilled treatment from a licensed clinician—more on that in a moment—but these pages *can* empower you with the beginning of a conversation between you and yourself (through reflection) or between you and your partner (if you're reading this together).

By the way, *Couples by Intention* (the book) isn't meant only for established couples. It's also for anyone trying to learn how to be intimate with someone else. The book is designed to open up new possibilities for you in your relationships, now or in the future, and to help you to imagine levels of intimacy you may not have known existed before. If you're single, the book can be a great resource for growing in your skill if and when you enter into your next committed relationship.

Whether you're single, seeing someone, or married, one thing is always true: intimacy is risky business. When we open ourselves up to the potential for deep rewards like companionship, connection, security, and sex, we're risking the possibility that we might get hurt along the way. Yes, we want to be viscerally connected to our partners, to know and expect their reactions, to learn to give them what they like in order to bring them pleasure, comfort, and love—to transition from just being "me" to creating an "us." But it's a huge gamble. Each party puts a whole lot of "self" on the table in the process, not knowing whether it'll pay off in the end. It's hard work, and it's only possible when both partners allow themselves to be vulnerable, to work intentionally for a higher understanding of the union between them. Both of them have to show up—or in other

> ▼
>
> **When we open ourselves up to the potential for deep rewards like companionship, connection, security, and sex, we're risking the possibility that we might get hurt along the way.**
>
> ▲

words, "us requires two." This book is designed to give you tools to strengthen the link between you and your partner—to deepen the "us" between you.

A few words of clarification before we start. First, this book assumes that you aren't in a violent or abusive relationship. If you are, please take the appropriate steps to create safety, and do it as soon as you possibly can. If you are feeling unsafe, call your police department, go to the local emergency room for assistance, or search the Internet on "domestic violence" for information on the resources available to you. This book is not intended to help you stop your partner from abusing you, so if you're being mistreated, then please, for your own sake, respect yourself with the dignity you deserve and get help immediately.

Second, *Couples by Intention* doesn't assume that every couple is in a hetero, binary, monogamous relationship, or that they want to be or should. I've written this book to dignify many types of intimate, adult relationships that people engage in together consensually, and the only assumption I'm making is that healthy, grown-up relationships need to be meaningful, full of deep connection, and built on mutual trust and openness if they are to flourish.

Lastly, what you're about to read isn't intended as a replacement for guided work with a credible therapist. Couple's therapy can be a gratifying and meaningful experience and serve as a doorway to growth and connection that you may not have even thought possible. This book will help to introduce you to some of the concepts that I share with my clients, but I need to be clear that reading this book doesn't and cannot replace real therapeutic help from an actual clinician in person. If you are having unsolvable problems in your relationship, then you need to go get help right away. Please don't try to use this book as a substitute.

As it is, many couples do everything they can to avoid couple's counseling. They think that there's a stigma attached to it, or that admitting the need for help may be like admitting a fragility in the relationship, a weakness that they wouldn't want anyone else to know about. In my line of work, people sometimes try to tell me that couple's therapy is the "fast track to divorce," an admission of complete failure and hopelessness. But the reality is that it's precisely *because* couples don't do their work earlier on, when there's still an actual relationship to work on, that so many of them find that there's no connection left between them by the time they do come in to talk about it.

Think of it this way: it's as though someone were trying to cultivate a garden, but they never spend time plucking up the weeds when they're tiny. By the time the gardener finally decides to deal with the problem, it's only because the garden has gotten so overgrown with weeds that it's really ugly to look at. But by now, the weeds are so huge that they've choked out the desired plants, and there might not be anything left to enjoy even if the gardener *can* get all the weeds out.

Counseling works the same way. It's best to deal with problems when they emerge, rather than letting them fester, which is why some of the healthiest couples come in for counseling even when they don't think there is anything particularly "wrong." It helps them deal with their unseen issues before they get out of hand, before they start sucking the nutrients out of the relationship.

Of course, there can come a time to get couple's therapy specifically to end a relationship with dignity and respect. But most couples find that successful therapy requires an intentional focus on improvement, in the hope that a relationship *can* be made better. Effective couple's work is done with a talented practitioner when there is still some element of meaningful connection, even if it doesn't feel positive or particularly fun at the time. By doing so, each partner may discover ways of connecting and being intimate that they never even thought to notice before, and the process can breathe new life into the relationship between them even when all seemed beyond saving.

▼

Growth only comes from getting messy

▲

For that matter, I often advise people to come to couple's work when things are going spectacularly between them, so that they can stretch! Growth only comes from getting messy, just like a garden only becomes more and more beautiful and full of life when someone is willing to get down in the dirt and pull weeds. If everything were comfortable and easy between us and our partners, we would never want to change. Being able to lean intentionally into our discomfort, with guidance and curiosity, can create meaningful change if it's done right. Once a relationship is dead, the best therapist in the world can't breathe life back into it again, so it's always best to seek help long before reaching that point.

This book deals with themes of growth and intentional challenge that partners can harness when they want to improve their connection, and it discusses how those themes show up in real relationships between real people. *Couples by Intention* is for people who come into my office and people for whom it's not practical to do so; for people who wish they could pick up the phone and call a sex therapist, and for people who have already gotten help and just want to grow another step; for couples who are thrilled with each other, and people who live with a sense of disconnectedness and sadness and don't even know that there is a different way of being in the world.

Throughout this book, you'll meet some of the couples I've worked with, and you'll see some of what they've accomplished with each other and why it was important for them. I'll share information about their backgrounds, their challenges, the conversations they had, and areas of growth that they discovered with each other.

The couples are real. To protect their privacy, I've changed their names, and some couples who have shared similar experiences have been folded together for readability or to make sure their identities are secure. But in all cases, the material of their stories is real, and I am honored to have been able to walk with them in their journeys closer to each other.

To do this work, you'll need to face your fears of change and allow the temporary discomfort that growth requires. For example, as you work through the material in this book, you may encounter situations that address your own story or some part of it, whether it relates to your own personal development as an individual or to your growth as a couple. To develop a strong relationship together, the individuals in the relationship must always be growing and developing. The work may require you to go back with intentional reflection and curiosity to ask yourself some challenging questions about your relationship history and the decisions and assumptions you carry, because as a rule, if you want your partner to be better in relationship, you yourself need to be better in relationship. Learning to go through the personal growth and development process with a partner who is experiencing the same type of development is, by definition, a moving target, and it can be disorienting, requiring a whole new set of skills. It can be confusing when you start to see aspects of your long-term partner that you never knew were there, and it can be a perplexing process when you start to try new ways of living and thinking within just yourself. But that's true with most worthwhile things in life, isn't it? New ways of being are often awkward—*until they become normalized* through practice, patience, and sustained effort.

The payoff can be incredible. Couples who do this kind of work often report reaching remarkable, profound closeness and intimacy of a sort that catches them by surprise—and that the hard work of introspection, conversation, and adjustment together was a small price to pay for the pleasures of connection that can come as a result. That's the journey that I hope you will join me for as we walk through these stories together.

My hope for you is the very same hope that I hold for the couples that come to my office: that you will find the best version of *you* as an individual, and the most *connected and secure* version of you as a couple. As you read, it will be your responsibility to discover what the final state of your relationship will look like, since no two people and no two relationships are quite alike. There is no one right way to be a couple. You have self-determination to choose who you want to be in your relationship and what you want your relationship dynamic to be. This book is structured to give you time to reflect on the state of your connection and what you want it to be, and it will give you questions to prompt reflection for understanding.

How to Use This Book

If You Want to Skip Around, Skip Around!

Couples by Intention is structured such that if you read it start-to-finish, you'll basically be "listening in" on a group of couples during their twelve-week journey of group therapy together. Naturally, the lessons will "build" over time, as the couples grow in their skills and have deeper and deeper conversations—so if you tend to gravitate toward stories and narratives, you might prefer to read the chapters in order.

But you don't have to! Maybe you simply want to learn more about the different definitions of the term "monogamy" and how to choose a good definition with your partner. If that's true, then by all means, *skip ahead* to Chapter 4, "Monogamy, Monogamish, and Nonmonogamy" and learn all you can!

Or if you're really passionate about learning how to integrate how you *act* with how you *feel and think* in your relationship, then be my guest: skip on ahead to Chapter 8, "Who Are You, Anyway?—Alignment." That's perfectly fine.

The point is, read this book in whatever order makes the most sense to you, whether you walk through it beginning-to-end, or whether you dance around from place to place.

Don't Skip the Exercises!

Whether you read straight through or skip around, make sure to pause to reflect. At various places in the chapters, I'll be offering you exercises that can be helpful for challenging yourself and for creating dialogue with your partner. If you want lasting change, take time to do the work. When an exercise comes up, resist the urge to plow through, and instead, stop reading and do the exercise. Doing so will help you to gain *so much more* for your development and your relationship than simply "listening to me talk" (reading without reflecting) could ever give you. Take some time to answer the questions I'll give. To do this, you'll want to . . .

Keep a Journal

I *strongly* recommend that you keep a "relationship journal" to record and reflect on the work you do in this book. Grab a simple notebook or composition book from your home or a neighborhood store. As you read, capture your thoughts, feelings, reactions, memories, hopes, dreams—anything that comes up for you as you hear these stories and think about your own development and your relationship. Even write down the ways you disagree with me! That's okay, and I can take it! Besides, a journal can be a terrific place to expand on the exercises in the book, and I'll be asking you to stop and reflect, so make sure to have one with you. It'll help you to make sure the conversation isn't one-sided and that you stay part of the process.

Make This Book Yours!

Since we're on the subject of talking back: it's absolutely fine to write in this book, and I encourage you to! Mark it up, highlight it, underline key parts, dog-ear the pages and get coffee stains on them—just make it *yours*. Interact with the book by writing and drawing in it. Doing so will actually help you to comprehend the concepts a lot more.

About Me

Lastly, a little about my own background. I grew up in the Boston area and worked in corporate America for a while after college. But becoming a parent has a way of changing one's priorities in life, and that was certainly true for me.

When my children started coming into the picture, I realized that I wanted more than almost anything else to raise my kids to be strong, confident, and aware of who they were as individuals. I wanted them to know about their emotions, their relationships, their bodies, and how to build meaningful lives in a chaotic world—and I knew that learning how to raise kids with those skills would push me beyond what I knew at the time.

I went back to school to study what makes relationships and emotional development "work," in part so that I could gain skill in coaching my kids through their development years, and they could safely and confidently discover who they were and how to relate well to those around them. Like I said at the beginning of this introduction, most of us don't get a class about relationships, and I knew that my kids weren't likely to have one, either. But I at least wanted to guide them well as a parent, and before I could teach them, I knew that I had to learn some things myself.

That's why I went to school again, and it's how I got the training to become a therapist—mostly because I wanted an idea of how to raise my kids well through their relational and emotional development. I decided to put what I was learning to use in my professional life as well, and today, many years later, I have a vibrant and full practice near my home in Boston.

Each week at my practice, I counsel individuals and couples as they work to build strong foundations for the future, and I look to create spaces and processes where couples can resolve their challenges and live more meaningful lives. In my office on a given day, my clients and I might work on issues ranging from identity, empty nesting, or infidelity, to sexual dysfunction/discordance, infertility, communication, low libido, lack of sexual awareness, and much more.

My work with couples has developed many themes that are consistent across the various types of work that I do with clients. For example, I've learned that as a rule, people want to feel more confident in their ability to be open with a partner, and they want to feel more secure in their skills and knowledge of sex: how it works, what to do, how to please a partner, how to ask for what they want, and so on. They also want to challenge the old messages about love, sex, and relationships that they have been carrying throughout their lives, often inherited from the generation before them. They want to be better communicators and listeners, and they want less conflict with their partners. Perhaps above all, they want to be seen and heard, both in the bedroom and out of it.

When I get to see partners learn how to do exactly that for each other—how to see, hear, and please each other, becoming stronger and more resilient in their love and their bond—those are the sweetest and most fulfilling moments for me in my day-to-day practice. My hope is that as you read the stories and do the exercises in *Couples by Intention,* you too will be encouraged to see how far and how strong your own relationships can become through careful, patient effort—to be inspired, like I have, by the astonishing couples you're about to meet.

One other person deserves a mention here, too: my grand-mother Annie. She was one of the most wonderful people I've ever met, and as I sit here at my desk in Boston, I can look out my office window and see the house where she lived, the place where she would tell me stories about connection, love, and relationship. Once, when I was in college and struggling to understand some relationships in my life at that time, she said something that has stuck with me all these years later, brilliant in its simplicity and profound in its impact on my life. She said, *Do your work now or do your work later, but everyone has to do their work. The longer you wait, the harder it is.*

▼

Do your work now or do your work later, but everyone has to do their work. The longer you wait, the harder it is.

▲

In many ways, her simple bit of insight has been the foundation for all my work with couples, in the hope that they can experience the joy of deep closeness and intimacy for themselves. I want that for you, too. And so now, I invite you to do your work.

First Steps–Setting the Scene for Getting Closer

In this chapter, you will:

- Meet two of the couples from my therapy group, which is called "Couples by Intention": Bradley and Carol, Sam and Yolanda

- Learn about setting realistic expectations for how to grow closer to your mate

- Eavesdrop on the first session of the group's time together and learn some of the ground rules:

    ◆ Confidentiality

    ◆ Couple-to-couple friendship isn't expected

    ◆ The No-Helping Rule

Picture a warm, cozy room with about a dozen seats arranged in a circle of sofas, loveseats, and comfy chairs. It's a Wednesday evening in autumn, and the light outside the window has started to fade into the gentle, dark blues and purples of the average New England school-night. As I erase what was left on the whiteboard from earlier in the day, a young couple comes in through the doorway, taking off their coats and greeting me with a familiar "Hi, Elliott" before choosing two seats beside each other. The couple's names are Bradley and Carol, and they're waiting for the other partner-pairs to arrive for the very first session of Couples by Intention, the therapy group that I offer at my practice near Boston.

The purpose of Couples by Intention is to provide some "shakeup" for couples who have been together for a while, creating pathways to better intimacy and connection by exposing avenues of communication and eroticism that they hadn't known were available within their relational system. During the course of their time together, the participants are challenged to face a variety of topics, such as how to create healthy boundaries around and within the relationship, and understanding the messages we get from parents and the world about sex, intimacy, and relationship role models, along with money, faith, parenting, listening, and how to manage change.

That's what Bradley and Carol are here to do, along with several other couples. Here is the story of their relationship, and the circumstances that brought them into our sofa-lined room on this particular evening.

Bradley and Carol

Bradley and Carol are both creative people in their mid-thirties. Smart and well-read, they had been college sweethearts before they got married. Now they have two small children and, by all outward indicators, a cohesive and collaborative marriage. Both partners are strongly opinionated, but soft-spoken and conflict-averse. Each identifies the other as their best friend.

Despite their strong outward relationship, sex and intimacy are a challenge for them, and they came to the therapy group not knowing how to talk about their issues but each strongly desiring better intimacy and sexual gratification.

Bradley wants sex but doesn't know how to ask for it.

He has been sober for more than ten years and has a great deal of shame when it comes to sex and addiction. He describes himself as "wearing a heavy cloak" that weighs him down so that he can't allow himself to be open to the joy of intimacy. His parents were deeply religious and avoided the topic of sex, and he never witnessed his parents showing intimacy or affection to each other. He is so focused on Carol's reactions that he forgets to tend to his own desires.

Carol wants connection, but she works so much that she is exhausted all the time. Carol's mother died when she was twelve, and as a result Carol had a challenging childhood that put her in a parental role at a very young age, helping to raise her younger brother. While Carol had a loving father, she became responsible for the household so that he could work. Carol feels great responsibility for everyone and strives to provide for everyone's needs—except her own. When it comes to sex and intimacy, Carol won't ask for what she wants, won't initiate, and often will report that just sitting in a bubble bath by herself is more gratifying than being intimate with Bradley.

Bradley and Carol were invited to Couples by Intention after participating in individual and couple's therapy that began shortly after Carol learned that Bradley had had a period of sexual infidelity at massage parlors. At the start of their couple's therapy, they hadn't been sure they would remain a couple, but through their individual work, both partners were able to focus on their own challenges to intimacy to a point where they had a strong understanding of the task before them. In the couples therapy, they began working on trust and creating a language in which they could explore their connection together. As their skills grew, they were better able to articulate their desires for a different type of relationship, one that was centered on a collaborative vision and allowed each of them to honor their unique journeys to each other. They became intentional, and began talking about and making forward movement toward a more connected relationship, one that included a meaningful sex life.

After displaying the courage to talk about their fears and hesitations, Bradley and Carol were able to return to why they wanted to be married to each other, and now they are actively working on their intimacy. While sex can still be challenging for both of them, Bradley and Carol each realize that they no longer have to hold to a formless, shapeless definition of what the right amount of sex is, or what kind of sex they're supposed to be having. As they continue to grow in their marriage, they are now finding meaningful ways of connecting that honor their unique ways of being together in a more open fashion.

Bradley and Carol give a perfect example of the trends I see in my couple's therapy practice day after day. The two of them were very committed to changing the dynamic of their marriage from one that was based on assumptions about themselves and each other to one that was based on trust and curiosity, but they had to do a ton of hard work and therapy to learn to communicate with each other and to love well, physically and otherwise. Couples by Intention was about to give them the chance to learn how.

First Impressions: Confidence and Jitters

I love it when couples are able to bring themselves into an environment that a group like Couples by Intention provides. It allows each participant and each couple to ask hard questions, use their curiosity, and get support to be the best version of themselves that they can. It isn't always easy. This can be fairly intimidating for some couples, since it involves putting their relationship "out there" publicly for other couples to see in earnest. Some couples, though, are eager to do the work and are quite open for the challenge, and many couples are shocked to discover that there is so much more to question and learn than they ever realized.

At the first session, we see that the group includes some couples and individuals who are completely charged up and ready to share. They want to get to know everyone, they want to start sharing stories about each couple's relationships, they're infectiously curious about what there is to learn, and they come with lots of humor and a willingness to self-disclose. They come to the first session with

▼

Many couples are shocked to discover that there is so much more to question and learn than they ever realized.

▲

coffee and cookies in hand, like they are going to a neighborhood block party. Before the group even officially starts, they introduce themselves to every person in the waiting room and make jokes with people about their baked goods. I can sense that some participants take great comfort in how these couples take the stigma out of the idea of group therapy.

Others are more conservative but warm quickly when they realize that couples besides their own have challenges and are able to talk about them. They tend to become strong advocates for questioning and probing for deeper meaning within the life of the group. They are often quiet and careful at first, but they become 100 percent engaged before very long. (We sometimes call that being "fully in the room.") You can see their energy rising as the conversation begins. During the formal introductions, they may start making connections with individuals, and you can see their bodies relax with the new familiarity, which can prompt others to relax in turn. It doesn't take long before they are ready to be active in the group.

There are also those group members who enter the first session so stressed and rigid that their tension is clear on their faces. They look painfully uncomfortable in their chairs and don't talk, other than to do the briefest of personal introductions. They don't come from a place of trust or comfort. They might even be attending as a gift or a concession for their partner who has asked or required that they attend. When they warm and open up—and they do, in time—they are able to create dramatic shifts in the conversation and to deepen the learning of the whole group. They might begin the first session by sitting tall and rigid, legs crossed, hands folded in their laps, perhaps fidgeting or playing with their hair, hardly ever speaking up. They might give only the bare basics as they introduce themselves, not sharing much beyond their names, perhaps not speaking at all in the first or second session, always the first ones out the door. But by the third session or so, they have usually begun to breathe and open up. It's always interesting for me to see the changing dynamics among the couples, the ways that they morph to new levels of comfort, self-awareness, and intimacy between the first session and week twelve. The change can be dramatic, as we'll see.

Journal Question

Pause for a moment and respond to these questions in your journal. (Don't have one? Make sure to pick one up as soon as possible, so that you can get the most out of this book!)

- How do you think *you* would feel about talking openly about your relationship with a group of strangers? Would you be:
    - ◆ Automatically engaged and easily talkative?
    - ◆ Or very uneasy and hesitant?
    - ◆ Or somewhere in the middle?
- Do you think that one reaction is better than another? Why or why not?
- How do you think your partner would feel? Why?

Strength in Numbers: Everybody's Imperfect

If I were to ask a dozen different people the questions in the journal exercise that you just did, I would hear a dozen unique responses.

Not everyone is at the same level of comfort with airing their relationship's laundry in front of other people. But *simply knowing* that not everyone is instantly comfortable airing their relationship's laundry in front of other couples can have a powerful effect of destigmatizing the process of getting therapeutic help at all. Couples often find that the knowledge that other clients are just as nervous or as imperfect as they are helps them to relax and receive the goodwill of the people around them in the circle.

The imbalance between the promise of growth and connection on the one hand, and the intimidation factor that couples experience when they first hear about the group on the other hand, exemplifies the core struggle in many relationships. We tend to want an idealized state of connection, one that feeds our soul and connects us together in unique and everlasting safety, fueled by powerful desire that is both sustained and fulfilled. But we are most often afraid to do the work required to get there. Why the hesitation? The reason is actually quite simple: to achieve that state of intimacy, we risk losing the state of things as they currently stand, including the good parts. When we step out of the status quo, we change it—which means that we can never step back into it. It's gone forever. We know this intuitively, and so we feel an impending sense of loss as we weigh whether to take the plunge into attempting something deeper.

Plus, there's no guarantee that it'll work. We might find that we're not capable of doing the work, that we have chosen the wrong partner, or that our partner won't do the work with us. That's one of the great things about the model we use in Couples by Intention: from the minute they walk into the room, the couples know, for one simple reason, that their partners will do the work with them: they showed up in the first place. Plus, they begin to learn from the other couples that there is no clear path to the future, so they get to create a path that is unique and different while being supported by the others in the circle. As a result, each person's capacity to do the work, to ask the hard questions, and to face the often confusing and challenging realities of being in a relationship, grows with each passing week that the group meets. By the end of the group process, the promises of deep, meaningful connection are no longer weighed down by the intimidation of doing the work, because they've seen some of the payoffs already. The couples almost always leave the group with an understanding of what the work looks like, and they carry a confidence that they can meet any challenges they'll face in the future.

Each group has five or six couples. They are strongly connected, but they stand at varying stages of relationship development. They might be married or not, have children or not, own homes or not. The important thing is that they are a strongly connected couple that is eager to learn about how to strengthen the bond between them. They meet once a week for 12 weeks in 90-minute sessions, discussing what it means to be "intentional" couples.

▼

On the first night, the couples want to see which couple is the best and which is the one most on the brink, each hoping it isn't *them*.

▲

It's fun to watch the change among the group members during that time. At the start of the series, the couples tend to sit next to their partners, quietly scoping out the others to see who is the most dysfunctional, almost like they are building a "ladder of dysfunction" to see who is at the top and who is at the bottom. On the first night, the couples want to see which couple is the best and which is the one most on the brink, each hoping it isn't *them*. Even the most connected couples often report that at the start of the group process, they are concerned about what flaws or cracks the group might reveal in their seemingly secure connection together. The anxiety is to be expected. Couples often don't realize what skills they need in order to reach the next point in their relationship, and it can be uncomfortable to hear their partner talk about it in the open. Anxiety is about fear, and in this case, it can relate to things that the couples don't yet understand or are unsure they can control. To hear one's partner ask for things like greater closeness, different kinds or varieties of intimacy, more communication, stronger co-parenting, better control over money, and so on, can create anxiety. As a result, over time, the group works together to normalize that anxiety and turn it into an opportunity for curiosity and exploration.

Here's how that sometimes looks. Because humans are pack animals by nature, we need to know who the alpha is and where we fit in the hierarchical order. The same is true when we couple. How many times have you found yourself comparing your relationship to those of your friends or coworkers? Often when someone talks about how great or awful their partner is, we get a natural inclination to identify how our relationship compares to how we perceive theirs to be. We are left with a wistful wish to be like them, or a grateful acknowledgment that we aren't. We are constantly putting ourselves and our relationships into the pecking order of relationship greatness.

Nobody's Perfect

But the truth is, every relationship has its ups and downs, its functions and its dysfunctions. When we are looking into our relationship—really looking—we begin to understand that we don't know everything about our partner, which can be a scary thought. After all, we're taught from an early age that we're supposed to know everything about our partner, and that successful relationships are based on knowing each other so well that we can predict what they think and how they will react. But those ideas don't actually hold true in healthy relationships, and besides, the need to be the best is an unnatural pressure that culture puts onto couples from the earliest stages of connection.

Culture tends to give us unhelpful messages about other aspects of relating, too, like gender. From our youngest ages, we start to learn how men and women are *supposed* to act and respond in relationships. Over the decades, many books have been published about Mars/Venus, Cinderella and Peter Pan complexes, and more. These tomes can be confusing and set expectations for behavior that aren't true to each individual's uniqueness and the ways each relationship is different from all others.

There is an even greater dissonance regarding gender messages when we identify as something other than the gender binary of male/female. There is not yet enough research and understanding to support expectations about what gender nonconforming, queer-identifying, trans, or other individuals of varying sexual orientations "ought" to experience as similar or different from straight couples when they form and grow deeply meaningful relationships. The lack of diversity in role models, research, supportive social structures, and more would make it disrespectful to state that the experience should be uniform among the diversity of types of relationships that are emerging.

Just the same, cultural expectations have been drilled in across generations and decades, and unless someone teaches us that we can be different from what society expects from men and women, we fall into those relationship stereotypes or spend a lifetime battling against them. Couples often struggle to know how to break through those conventions and actually "show up" to each other in ways that allow them to know each other in their diversity and uniqueness.

Plus, there's a tacit expectation in our culture that we have to be *awesome* at relating. Messages from Disney, romantic comedies, novels, faith communities, and any number of other pop-culture sources tell us that once we commit, we must be the *best* couple, and any perceived flaws are seen as inherent signs that something is wrong with the relationship or with us. We carry those ideas forward into how we relate to the ones we love. But those expectations can only bring a heightened sense of disillusionment once we inevitably realize that our relationships aren't perfect and that when two people get close, things tend to get messy and broken along the way.

The Fire Cools

Typically, at the beginning of a relationship, we are at our very best, knowing that if we want the relationship to continue and thrive, we have to be on our best behavior, remain pleasant and cool, and try to keep the other's attention. There aren't any guarantees that the other person will show up for a second date, that they will return texts or calls, what they are going to wear or what they'll want to talk about. That lack of knowing, that sense that nothing is certain about the future of the relationship, is a hook. Anticipation can be exciting! We are open to each other, allowing ourselves the space and time not to know everything about our partner. In those earliest stages, any connection at all can feel dramatic and huge, and we begin to feel confident with every tiny bit of awareness of our partner that we gain.

That was the case with Bradley and Carol. They described their earliest relationship moments as fun and curious. Both of them prioritized their relationship above school, work, and friends. They were smitten with each other and wanted to get to know each other. In session, each of them was able to share memories of how they tried to impress upon each other that they should keep the relationship going. In other words, Bradley and Carol were at their most pliable and hopeful, full of anticipation and a willingness to be open.

But the period of deep learning and openness usually doesn't last long. Once we start feeling comfortable, the gift of being able to *not know* starts to diminish. The window of being okay with ignorance about our partner starts to close, and we start to assume that we know so much about him or her that we don't need to pay attention with the same focus and energy. Socially, we start to present to others that we are strongly connected because, well, we want others to think that we *are* strongly connected. The reason is simple: those around us, such as our friends and family, are *also* being affected by the same implicit lessons from pop culture, like the pressure to have a perfect relationship. Everyone's sense of pressure and desire not to appear as failures begins to reinforce each other's insecurities, and *every* relationship in a social circle can suffer in some way, a domino effect of perceived pressures to perform.

Bradley and Carol experienced this as well. As they began to get socially recognized as a couple, friends and relations started inviting them to hang out, with the expectation that the +1 meant the other person: getting Bradley was understood to mean getting Carol, and vice versa. "I'm not sure why, but people just assumed Carol and I were getting married," said Bradley once. "No one asked me if that was what I wanted. They asked me *when* we were getting married. Everywhere I went.

"The same with kids. Once everyone knew how much I liked Carol and that we were really doing this relationship thing, I got put on this ridiculous track that I couldn't get out of. It was confusing, because it kinda felt great to be acknowledged as a guy that could land someone like Carol, but it also began to piss me off. What kind of asshole would I be if I just started talking about other things I wanted for me that didn't include Carol? I knew what was being expected of me."

Bradley and Carol's experience of social pressure shows what's typical in our culture and serves as an illustration of what countless couples experience every day. If we don't have strong and positive prior relationship experience, the situation often becomes even worse. This is because without positive prior relationship experience, we may not even know how to check into what is really going on with our partner, or we may be fearful of what we might find out if we do check in. What happens if we find out something we don't know how to handle? What if we learn that the assumptions we have been acting on are wrong, and we have to adjust our whole approach to our partner? The longer the relationship continues, the harder it is to challenge our assumptions and understandings—so the more we wait to ask, the greater the risk feels and the greater the disincentive to learn more about our partner! After all, we have invested immense amounts of time and energy just to get to *this* point—so who would want to risk it?

That's part of why joining a group like Couples by Intention is such a courageous act in and of itself. Even to show up for the first session, each individual has to take the bold step of challenging their own assumptions about themselves and their partner. Then, once they're in the group and some momentum has been established over a few weeks, couples start to realize that there is a level playing field, because all of them are the healthiest in some dimension of relating, and more challenged in another, and *which* couple is the "best" at any given element keeps changing with the topic of conversation. The "ladder of dysfunction" turns out not to really exist after all.

We're All In This Together

In time, realizing that everyone is imperfect helps the group members open up to one another. By the third week, with no intervention from me, the members of each couple aren't even sitting together anymore, choosing instead to inter-mingle with each other. Some weeks, the women are on one side of the room and the men on the other, which creates an interesting dynamic on its own as partners begin talking to their counterparts across the room as much as they speak to the other couples. Couples begin to challenge themselves by questioning their status quos and stating their truth: that they want more connection, more intimacy, more sex! And as cross-talk starts to emerge among the members of the group, some other dynamics start to come out as well. Younger couples remind older

▼

Couples begin to challenge themselves by questioning their status quos and stating their truth: that they want more connection, more intimacy, more sex!

▲

couples that fun and excitement should be more frequent, but they are hungry for guidance and wisdom, which the older couples start to provide eagerly. Couples that are in their first major relationship learn from those who have been divorced or have created blended families. Straight couples, gay couples, and nonbinary couples learn about their commonalities and their uniqueness from each other, enriching the entire conversation as the collective wisdom of everyone gathered gets shared around the room.

Each 90-minute session ends with a period of reflection and what we call "naming the growth." For ten minutes at the end, I ask the group to reflect on questions like these: What will you keep doing? What will you start doing? What will you stop doing? And what will you think more about?

Then, before we part for the night, each person shares their response to one or more of the questions above. It usually sounds something like, "What Yolanda said about . . . really made me think about . . . " or, "I really like how Bradley and Carol . . . " or, "I never realized that we . . . " You'll encounter some of these stories in the chapters that follow, and each chapter of this book will close by guiding you through an exercise of answering these questions for yourself.

By the end of the twelve weeks, the couples report that they are more open in how they engage each other, and that their intimacy and sex are better, deeper, and closer. Plus, the couples have built a strong network of support and encouragement with each other, and many stay in touch after the group has ended. I have even had groups request to have periodic group meetings in my office to continue the mutual aid and support work that they have created together.

The Importance of Being Ready

It's important that participants in the Couples by Intention process all have a high degree of commitment to working on their relationship and are experienced enough to challenge themselves and their partner in a manner that doesn't create undue anxiety. Sam and Yolanda, another young couple in the group, had demonstrated a willingness to be open to what their partner brought to the group as an opportunity to be better and stronger as a couple. As the facilitator, it's important that I have a high degree of confidence in their skill to handle the conversations and reactions they and their partners will experience as topics and issues come up. The group is successful when each participant and each couple can go home and have the excited, engaged, challenging, and curious discussions that arise from the experience of sitting with each other and looking at their own dynamics honestly.

Here's a glimpse of what Sam and Yolanda had been through together before Couples by Intention started.

Sam and Yolanda

Sam, 32, and Yolanda, 26, are a young couple, having dated for three years and lived together for two. They met at work when they were both seeing other people, but before long, they both found themselves single at the same time, and they described an "instant spark."

Sam had been engaged before but called off the wedding when he realized that his ex-fiancée did not seem to have the same dreams for the future. After that traumatic experience, Sam was a bit hesitant to get back into a deeply committed relationship—until he met Yolanda. As to his sexuality, Sam likes sex but often feels a lower-than-normal libido and is unlikely to initiate.

Yolanda is an only child of immigrants. She lives with a variety of medical complications that make day-to-day life challenging. She describes herself as a "warrior" in her fight for her health, and she reports that Sam is her greatest champion. Because of her medical complications, sex and intimacy are often a challenge for her. That's not to say that she doesn't have a healthy libido and desire: she has both. To meet her need, she has a collection of sex toys that she enjoys using with or without Sam.

Both partners struggle with having a language to talk about sex, desire, and fantasy. They came to the group wanting to learn how to be more open with communication and to normalize their physically challenging sex life, and they reasoned that it would be helpful to learn how other couples navigate the landscape of sex and intimacy.

There's another reason for their joining the group, too. As a result of Yolanda's health care concerns, fertility is a major challenge, and they will most likely need to use third-party reproduction such as IVF, or possibly an egg donor and surrogate. Yolanda and Sam brought a unique perspective to the group, because they'd never had the romantic notion that they would just wake up pregnant one day and share the news with excitement and wonder with their inner circle of friends and family. They were painfully aware that any family-building would be as a result of multiple trips to a clinic, and they hoped that by coming to the group, they might be able to prepare themselves emotionally to support each other through the journey.

Sam and Yolanda are great examples of a couple that wants to do this work precisely *because* they know that there are gains to be made in their relationship, and they want the tools to achieve them. It's common that each partner in the couple has a different set of needs and skills, and that each has their own area of desired growth. Coming to my couple's group is about the ability to discover multiple ways of being a strongly connected, intimate couple. The couples who come understand that there is no single right way to achieve that goal. As I tell participants, I am happy that they come to the group, but the real learning is what happens after we have our discussion and they've gone home together. I encourage them to talk at home about what they've learned and to look to see how they will be different based on their interactions within the group. In other words, our sessions serve as a launchpad for the work they will do when they return home seeking to be different.

Being on the Same Page: Ground Rules

There are only a few rules that each individual and couple must agree to at the start of the group process. The first rule is that we must have a *commitment to confidentiality*, that what is said in the group stays within the group and never leaves the room. The type of work we do is deeply personal and intimate, and group members wouldn't be able to participate at the same level of self-awareness and discovery if safety weren't an absolute guarantee. If any parties from the group choose to connect together outside of our sessions, that's fine, but there is an agreement that the work and conversations from the group remain private and confidential.

The second rule is that *no one is expected to form friendships* with the other couples. No one is required to join together outside of the group, and there is no expectation of commitment to anyone but one's partner when the season has ended. True, every group so far has resulted in the couple's wanting to stay connected due to the deep safety and intimacy that is created by the process, but it's never an expectation or a requirement.

The third rule is the most important, and it's one that I implement in my couple's therapy sessions as well. It's the *"No-Helping*

Rule," and each person has to agree to abide by it before we begin our first session. A rule with a name like that may sound counterintuitive, especially since our desired goal is to create the conditions for each couple to become more connected to each other. But the reality is that helping each other is often what leads to the most trouble in relationships.

The No-Helping Rule

"Helping" can take many forms, but we define it generally to refer to one person taking an action for the benefit of someone else, whether out of generosity or habit. For example, when my partner picks up my coffee cup in the morning and puts it in the dishwasher, that's helping. The intention may be as generous as wanting to empower me to get out the door for work as efficiently as possible, but if I'm not finished with my cup, then it isn't helpful at all, and it can actually be the opposite of helpful. For example, if I have asked my partner before to leave my coffee cup alone, but it ends up in the dishwasher, my partner's "help" actually becomes an act of disrespect, not kindness. This shows that sometimes the simple act of helping in the way that we have all been taught can have negative consequences.

In session, "helping" looks like trying to usher people through difficult feelings by attempting to get them to stop crying or to calm down. One of our core values in Couples by Intention (and in my couple's therapy sessions) is that just because someone is experiencing a difficult or challenging emotion, it doesn't mean that they can't handle it, or need anyone's help to get through it, or even want to stop experiencing it. Often, when someone is feeling a difficult emotion, it's more difficult for the people *witnessing* it than for those *experiencing* it. It's the discomfort of the witness that can lead the witness to try to squelch the display. Being creatures who like feeling that we're in control of our circumstances, the faster we can get people to control themselves emotionally, the faster we can get back to what feels normal and safe. But some of the most important growth in session, as in the rest of life, happens when we feel uncomfortable enough to want to change, and some of the best

▼

**"Helping"
may interrupt
people's growth,
so we make
a deliberate
commitment
on the very first
night to get out
of each person's
way.**

▲

communication takes place when we're being our most authentic selves with those who love us. "Helping" may interrupt people's growth, so we make a deliberate commitment on the very first night to get out of each person's way, allowing them to experience whatever emotions and breakthroughs they need to in order to gain ground in their ability to relate.

Sometimes helping happens in our own heads when we actively avoid a difficult conversation or situation because we think the other person will collapse under the weight of the experience or have a strong negative emotion. How many times have you avoided a conversation that you wanted to have because you thought your partner would not be able to handle the gravity of it? Avoiding a conversation to avoid the conflict is, itself, a form of helping! It means that you are making the decision for your partner about what they can or should handle. But when you take the decision away from your partner, you are actually hurting your partner by "helping" them. It's important to note, though, that deciding to hold off on a conversation for a later time because it would be more compassionate or more meaningful or because you need more time is not considered helping. The key is to learn the difference. Helping happens when one person influences the other without permission, thereby overstepping a boundary.

This is different from *supporting*, which is welcomed and remains within established boundaries. Supporting happens when we create an environment where people can do the emotional work they need to do. The ability to witness someone's struggle in a supportive way can be a powerful act of kindness, and it requires being patient and generous. If the other person is doing their work, then it's about *them*. Being able to ask questions like, "What would you like to happen?" or, "What does that mean to you?" can often be a supportive way of allowing the other person to work through the challenge they are experiencing. But it's not the same as *helping*, because we're not trying to do the work *for* them.

Think about your own relationship for a minute. Would you

want people to assume you need them to tell you how to feel, what to say, how to make decisions? Of course not. But having an acknowledgment from your partner that yes, things are hard, can be quite meaningful. It just needs to stop at that point and not spill over into "helping."

Helping is rooted in dangerous assumptions that we usually don't even realize we are making. For example, when we "help," we are assuming that we know better than the other person does, that we are more capable than they are, they they need us, that they are lower in skill than we are. When we "help" in this way, we are actually inserting ourselves into a position of power over them and diminishing their own agency in the situation. While we wouldn't say such things out loud in healthy relationships, they can operate behind the scenes to some degree in nearly every couple, though not in every situation.

Learning to manage our own emotions and relationships happens only through experience. To grow and develop, we must face challenges and struggle to learn how to cope with them so that our resilience and insight can grow and deepen. When we "help" others, we rob them of the ability to do their work of growth and development. Ultimately, we must ensure that our comfort, anxiety, or avoidance do not inhibit the people we care about, especially our partner.

Exceptions

As with any rule, there are exceptions, and this rule has two. The first is that *if help is requested, it can be granted.* But in order to help, one's partner has to *ask* for help. The request can come in any form, but it should be concrete and specific, and before anyone agrees to help, they must understand exactly what is going to be expected. This is because we often agree to help without knowing what the other person's expectation is, and if we don't help in the way that is expected, we can get ourselves and our relationship into hot water. Imagine, for example, the frustration that could result if the "help" that is expected is for Bruce to read Brenda's mind and do the laundry, and that the help that Bruce offers instead is to leave Brenda alone and give her space and time. Brenda is going to become upset with Bruce for not reading her mind, and Bruce will become angry at Brenda for not expressing herself and rejecting the gift he tried to give! This exact situation is a common form of "helping" disconnect, and it gets lots of partners into trouble. It's why the request for help needs to be explicit, clear, and understood by both parties in advance.

The second exception is that *if help is offered, it can be accepted.* A partner can offer help at any time, but the offer must be specific and time-limited. If you are not crystal-clear about what you are willing and able to do for your partner, you might be expected to go further than your time, energy, and limits will allow, which could result in even greater discord.

It's also important to know that just because help is accepted or granted does not mean that there is a "carte blanche" between the two partners. For example, if Sam requests help from Yolanda to bring the groceries in from the car, it doesn't mean that Sam can also expect Yolanda to salt the stew pot and start chopping vegetables without asking for that, too. If Bradley offers to help Carol fold the laundry, it doesn't mean that Bradley is also offering to clean the bathroom.

Ultimately, the No-Helping Rule is about creating clarity in relationship boundaries so that each partner knows exactly what the rules are. This rule is in no way meant to allow partners to stop caring or paying attention. In fact, if the No-Helping Rule is implemented well, each partner is paying greater attention through the creation of supportive environments, patience, and clear, concise, explicit communication.

Journal Questions

The No-Helping Rule

Time to pause for a few minutes, break out your journal—did you make sure you have one?—and spend a few minutes jotting your answers to these questions:

1. Think about your relationship, and the definition of

"helping" that we've described. How does your partner "help" you that you find troubling?

2. How do you "help" your partner? When are you most likely to "help" without being aware of it?

3. How might your relationship be strengthened if you were to limit the amount of helping in your relationship?

Everybody Tries to Help Sometimes

In the group, helping often takes the form of trying to support others who are experiencing strong emotions by hugging them or giving them a "there, there" response out of concern that the emotion is too strong to manage. But instead, under the No-Helping Rule, participants start to learn that if a group member is sharing a difficult emotion, they can ask any member of the group for assistance if they need or want it, and anyone else can *offer* to help to see if it's desired. An offer of help might sound like, "Would you like a hug?" or, "Is there something you need right now?"

Helping can also take the form of giving advice when it hasn't been invited. In our group sessions in Boston, we might see this kind of helping take place when someone is struggling and another group member tries to advise them on how to solve their problem. The group is "helping" when I hear language like, "What you should do is . . . " or, "The right thing would be . . ." When I witness this behavior happening in the group, I call it out. I ask the person having the emotion or struggle if they know what the emotion is about (they nearly always do) and if they think they can handle it (again, they nearly always do). I gently remind the others that the struggle is the pathway to growth. When a group member is frustrated or working through a challenging situation, it is important that the other group members not take it as an invitation to *teach*. The teaching moment is a clear attempt to help, and it reinforces the dangerous assumptions of, "I know better than you do," "you can't do this without me," and "if I don't teach you my reality than you can't be as good as I think you can and should be."

This type of helping can happen outside of our sessions, too, and everyday life is filled with examples of stories of people giving unsolicited advice. Many of us have had experiences of being told what to do when all we needed was simply to "vent" our feelings or frustration, or to be heard without judgment by a friend who knows how to listen. If you've ever been annoyed by a friend who responds to your headache by telling you how to change your diet, or if you've ever had a stranger offer parenting advice when your baby is crying in public, you have experienced this kind of "helping" firsthand. Many of us have also "helped" our friends and loved ones in ways like these without meaning to, not realizing that our attempt to be helpful was only making our friend or loved one feel worse. That's why learning to spot the risk of offering to "help" *before* it actually happens is an essential relationship skill, and why the No-Helping Rule is such an important part of our group sessions at my practice. For many of my clients, it's the first time they've had to think of the effects their "helping" can have on those around them.

The rule may sound daunting or hard-nosed, but what's fascinating is how fast the group connects with it. Once group members allow themselves to notice when they want the others to help them and when (mostly) they really don't, it becomes easier for the whole group to observe the No-Helping Rule. This rule is also the start for creating a meaningful language within the group, a vocabulary that promotes equality and respect. When helping stops, everyone is on an equal footing. This is because every group member starts to operate from the assumption that every other member is capable of the work, and can be full and productive members of their relationship without the need for hand-holding from the people around them.

The No-Helping Rule became a starting point for huge growth one night when Amy, one of the group members, became emotional describing how her overall stress was driving a wedge in her relationship. "I try to manage my stress," she said, "but I just turn into a raving bitch sometimes and I hate it. My husband hates it. My kids hate it, and I begin to think they hate me too."

"I don't think you are a bitch," piped up Matt, her husband. "But man, some days your stress wears me out. I know you are trying, and that helps."

At this, Amy began to weep openly. Immediately wanting to ease Amy's pain, Seema, another woman in the group, said, "I think you should try yoga. It always seems to center me when I am having a tough day." But I jumped in and reminded Seema that this constituted helping: Amy wasn't asking for anyone in the group to tell her how to manage her stress. She was simply sharing the awareness of the impact of her stress on her life and the lives of her loved ones.

Ultimately, it was Seema who had the greatest learning in the moment. "Oh my god," she said, taken aback when she realized what had happened. "I do this all the time! I'm always trying to manage everybody else's life. I just can't resist. My family doesn't listen to me—and it's because I'm not listening to them!"

▼

"My family doesn't listen to me—and it's because I'm not listening to them!"

▲

This moment allowed the group to confirm for Amy that she actually did have the ability to manage her interactions with her family, and that Matt was able to see that she had a deep self-awareness. It allowed him to continue being supportive. Seema, too, identified an area of personal growth that her partner and family had hoped she would learn. Everybody won—and it came through one group member needing to be gently corrected for trying to "help" another.

Looking Back, Looking Ahead

In this chapter, we've introduced several members of the Couples by Intention group, and we've described why we have the group in the first place and what we're trying to accomplish: taking partners who are willing to do the hard work of learning how to grow closer together and leading them just a little further in their development as a couple.

We've also looked at our three ground rules:

1. confidentiality,
2. no expectation of friendship between couples, and
3. the No-Helping Rule.

We also talked extensively about what the No-Helping Rule means and why "helping" can be harmful.

We'll spend more time getting to know the couples in the course of the next few chapters. In Chapter 2, we'll talk about how couples can take their first steps in becoming *intentionally* intimate.

But first, it's time to do some reflecting.

Journal Questions

Chapter 1 Reflections

Now that you've finished Chapter 1, pull out your journal again and respond to these questions before moving on to the next chapter. Having read through Chapter 1:

1. What will you *keep doing* in your life and relationship that you are already doing?
2. What will you *start* doing, based on what you learned?
3. What will you *stop* doing?
4. What will you *think more about?*

Have a Reason–Be Intimate on Purpose

In this chapter, you will:

- Meet more of the couples in Couples by Intention
- Learn about why intimacy can diminish over time, and how to keep it alive
- Think carefully about what we mean when we say "intimacy"
- Discover the power of swagger and the importance of choice

In Chapter 1, we sat with some of the Couples by Intention members as they explored their first-week jitters and started getting more comfortable with one another. Before we go further, I want to tell you a little about what some of the couples had done *before* they came to group therapy. We'll step back in time to look at some of the therapy work I do with partners before they're invited to Couples by Intention.

To begin, let's hear John and Meili's story.

John and Meili

John, 31, and Meili, 30, are a married, biracial couple without children. They came to therapy to work through a complex set of childhood experiences that were bound by very different cultural norms and messages about love, sex, and marriage. These experiences were inhibiting their ability to feel like they were working together for a unified future.

John worked a job that he found to be less than gratifying, and he reported feeling tortured every day. He would frequently comment that he felt inadequate and ineffective. He had been brought up in a strict family that had high expectations for his academic and professional performance, which he felt he was not meeting. As a result, he was experiencing a strained relationship with his family of origin and reported a challenged sense of his own manhood. Because no one ever talked to him about sex, everything he learned was via the Internet, through porn, and from friends. He reported that partner sex was hard to talk about. Because of his lack of confidence, he wouldn't initiate sex with Meili, and he relied heavily on porn and masturbation to meet his erotic needs.

Meili's mother died in a car crash when Meili was almost ten. As the only daughter, she was thrust into a maternal role at a very young age. Her father was overwhelmed, and she would later describe him as cold but caring. This made Meili very focused on independence and her career and gave her a heightened sense of personal responsibility. She has developed an extremely high standard for herself and John. He knows it, and his struggle to achieve it often reinforces his perceived lack of manhood. Likewise, because John doesn't meet her standards, Meili doesn't feel receptive toward sex or intimacy with him. She also reports great anger about John's porn use, viewing it as an infidelity.

John and Meili were invited to the group after

participating in couple's therapy. Having worked through the emotional crisis of John's porn use and creating a basic language that allowed them to talk about strong emotions, John and Meili wanted to attain a level of comfort in how they planned for the future and problem-solved together. They spent a great deal of time in therapy prior to joining the group, learning to talk about how they wanted to be treated. Both partners wanted to talk more openly about the realities of their life and their desire to have children, even though sexual intimacy was still a challenge.

When I work with couples, either in couple's therapy or in a group setting like Couples by Intention, I spend a great deal of time at the start setting up a common language and understanding, a foundation on which we can build. It's important to understand what we mean when we use important terms like *intimacy* and *intention,* and it's crucial that each group member know what expectations and unique influences they bring into a relationship, and how those things become either building blocks or roadblocks. This chapter is focused on helping you to create a foundation for the work that's coming later.

Why Intimacy Dies

I had a client who had been desperately seeking love and connection. Caitlin was a single woman who arrived at her session infuriated. I had barely gotten to my chair to start the session when she began to rant.

"So, I am on a date Friday night," she said, "and I'm with this guy who had messaged me online. We'd chatted for a bit online last week and I'd asked him if we could move this 'thing' offline. I hate when you start chatting with someone online and it gets stuck there, sending messages but never getting any forward traction. So I asked him if we could talk on the phone.

"The call went okay," she continued, "and he asked me if I wanted to catch a drink after work Friday night. So, I made sure I wore something nice, and I was really excited all day. I met him at the bar. He seemed okay and it was all going well, until he picked up his phone. Get this: he pulled up my profile and said, 'In your profile you have brown hair.' I told him that I did and that I just went to the salon to get highlights. He said, 'Sorry, I don't really like redheads,' and he dropped twenty bucks on the table and left!

"I was speechless!" she fumed. "I'd just spent a lot of money on my highlights! I really love my highlights, and they're more copper than red anyway!"

Caitlin's experience was a sad example of something that is becoming more and more common. The creation of intimacy in the earliest stages of relationships is under an enormous challenge because of how powerful Internet- and app-dating have become. The movement from traditional dating to online and electronic dating has shifted our assumptions about dating and the process of getting to know another person. In earlier generations, you had to get personally involved with another human being in order to get a date. You actually had to *talk* to someone you wanted to get to know better. Perhaps a friend would introduce you to someone, or maybe you'd meet a coworker at an event for the first time, or perhaps you'd simply go up to someone and ask for a date (or maybe someone came to *you*).

> **Online dating has turned the entire dynamic of human engagement on its head.**

Much of that has changed now. Online dating has turned the entire dynamic of human engagement on its head. Electronic engagements have made potential partners into commodities. Having the cache of dating options available in the palm of our hands means that we can swipe right or swipe left with little or no information about who people are inside: "Here's a picture of Dave, and he's wearing flannel. Don't like flannel? Swipe left. Goodbye, Dave." "Here's a picture of Jennifer. Don't like her eye color? Breasts too big or too small? Swipe left. Tough luck, Jennifer."

This mentality and flexibility work *against* us as we try to create intimate connections because many of us have lost the expectation that we must work actively at making and maintaining a relationship. I have spent more hours in my office challenging people to slow down than I can count, trying to convince them to allow a bit of curiosity into their dating approach in the hopes that they will be able to find a start of some meaningful intimacy that can grow and build a more substantial connection.

John and Meili had first come to therapy long before Couples by Intention because they felt they didn't understand intimacy at all. They were good friends, but they had very different approaches to their lives, and they were having trouble reconciling their two ways of being. John tended to be fairly passive, while Meili was a strong and vibrant doer. When they first started dating, their individual styles seemed to complement each other. John appreciated having a partner with strong opinions. It made him feel like he wasn't holding all the responsibility for planning and executing plans—just the way he liked it. Meili, for her part, enjoyed being with a man who didn't challenge her. Thanks to her many years of being an authority in her house even in childhood, she was used to being in charge, and she didn't like to get into authoritarian battles. John's passivity felt like a breath of fresh air for her, at least at first.

Over time, the combination of Meili's strong presence and John's laid-back approach to life and relationships led to an imbalance in how they each showed up in their relationship. Where Meili had previously seen John as one who wouldn't get in the way, eventually she started to see him as someone who wouldn't "show up" at all, who wasn't holding up his end of leadership. It started to become a source of tension and resentment for Meili, because she didn't *want* a subservient worker: she wanted a full partner, someone who *could* challenge her. Over on John's side, things weren't much better. Whereas at first, John had seen Meili as a strong-willed leader, he started seeing her as a controller, a judge, and an unhappy boss, constantly complaining about his perceived failure to step up. This only triggered John's challenged sense of manhood inherited from his family of origin, and spiraled him further into insecurity. By the time they came to therapy, they were describing their feelings in the language of hurt and confusion, of dashed hopes for how their life would be. How could it have felt so great in the beginning of their relationship, and yet feel so miserable now? Had they really changed that much? Had they been blind to what was really in front of them when they had first started going out? Had they simply stopped caring and gotten lazy?

The confusion that John and Meili were facing was not unique to them, and in fact, Sam and Yolanda had been dealing with similar confusion. As Yolanda's health became more challenged, Sam reported that he felt their relationship was better than it had been, but he couldn't put his finger on why. Yolanda had less capacity to help around the house, her mood was more erratic, and she couldn't always go to work, which meant that Sam had to do more work around the house and live more independently from Yolanda, and they had less sex. So why on earth, Sam wondered, was their relationship actually *improving*? Yolanda felt the same way. Life was getting harder, but their relationship seemed to be growing stronger and stronger, like a bedrock under their challenges. But she was at a loss to explain it.

What Do You Mean by "Intimacy"?

There are as many definitions for intimacy as there are people, so when someone is in my office, one of the first things I ask them is for their definition of intimacy. Some of the most common responses I hear include:

- ➤ marriage
- ➤ sex
- ➤ how we feel about each other
- ➤ trust
- ➤ talking
- ➤ touch
- ➤ relationship
- ➤ unattainable
- ➤ the indescribable feeling
- ➤ being comfortable with another person

- confusing
- secrets we share
- cuddling
- scary
- "I don't know!"

I am always confirmed that people "get" intimacy but don't know how to *describe* it. I often find it better to let them struggle with finding a definition rather than "helping" them to mine. In this way, intimacy is like the way Supreme Court Justice Potter Stewart famously described porn: people tell me that they know intimacy when they see it, even though they can't explain exactly what it is. But there's a problem with a definition that loose. If *you* can't explain what you mean by intimacy, then your *partner* doesn't know what you want or even whether they're sharing it with you. And then how would you go about articulating the definition of intimacy that your partner uses? What is your partner looking for in terms of intimacy? And are you sure that you're looking for the same thing?

> **If *you* can't explain what you mean by intimacy, then your *partner* doesn't know what you want or even whether they're sharing it with you.**

When I ask these questions initially, I do so to get an assessment of the core messages about intimacy that people have received over their lifetime. In many ways, our ideas about intimacy are bound up in the cultures that each of us come from. Intimacy in Asian cultures, for example, tends to look different from intimacy in African-American cultures. Messages about restriction and suspicion of the body that derived from Victorian England are very different from the messages from some more body-positive messages that some other cultures have given the world. Each community's approach to intimacy has grown from a unique combination of messages and values across the generations.

In the U.S., we experience intimacy and closeness differently in different regions of the country. Southern propriety demands a certain social self-consciousness and manner in talking about sex and intimacy, which is very different from the New England way of talking about them that tends to be more open, although hints of its roots in Puritanism come out from time to time. Issues such as faith, education, economics, politics, and others influence the way that children, and the adults they become, talk about, understand, and engage in sex and intimacy.

It's no wonder that by the time someone is sitting on my office couch in a therapy session, such a seemingly simple question as, "What is intimacy?" gets such a blank, bewildered response! Having seen it happen hundreds, perhaps thousands, of times in my practice, I'm convinced that we owe it to ourselves to unpack the seemingly simple, often complex understandings of intimacy that we carry with us.

Understanding the messages we have received in our lifetime can reduce the chance that we'll be *reactive* around our partner and increase the likelihood that we'll be *intentional* in how we try to be intimate. When I ask people how they learned about intimacy, they are often perplexed by the question, as though they assumed that the knowledge just fell into them in a mystic or automatic way. Usually, they've never thought even to ask the question, so I encourage them to stop and think:

➤ How *did* you learn about intimacy?

➤ What was the message?

➤ Where did it come from?

➤ How was it displayed?

➤ Was it positive and reaffirming, or was it negative and shaming?

➤ How did religion, financial stability, birth order, gender, sexual identity, and other factors influence the messages you received?

➤ How many of those messages aligned with each other, and which ones conflicted? Did the messages they received at home as a child align with those from school and peers? How did those messages differ from what you learned in the movies, television, social media, and literature?

➤ How did you sort them out?

Journal Questions

Intimacy Exercise 1—Your Messages about Intimacy

Time to stop for a few moments, dust off your journal, and write some answers to these questions: Think about the word "intimacy." How did you learn about what intimacy is? Who taught you? What examples of intimacy have you seen in your life? Think about the sources and the messages you received from your family and culture, either positive or negative, and write your answers in your journal.

Examples:

1. **Source:** Grandpa Jim and Grandma Iris

   Message: They were always flirting with each other, and they made no secret of when they wanted to be behind closed doors together, even at age 85

2. **Source:** My friend Justine

   Message: If a couple doesn't have sex at least twice a week, one of them is probably having an affair

3. **Source:** My family's culture

   Message: Intimacy is no one's business except the husband and wife, so I grew up never thinking or talking about intimacy, and now I feel clueless

4. **Source:** My church

   Message: Talking about bodies or sex is very wrong. If you are curious or doing something about it, you should be ashamed

Those are just examples. Make this your own! Try to come up with at least 4 or 5 if you can.

Using the Same Vocabulary

Think back to the stories you've read about Carol (from Chapter 1) and Meili (from this chapter). These two women shared the common experience of having been raised without a strong mother figure. Both women also had fathers who were dedicated and committed to raising their children, but due to their own lack of information and insight, they were unable to model positive relationship intimacy for their daughters. Both women came to the Couples by Intention therapy group as strong, vital women who struggled to translate their strength and self-confidence into openness, and they each experienced intimacy challenges in their relationships as a result. They each had a strong sense that they could have been setting a better example for their daughters to follow if only they had had a better working knowledge—a bigger "vocabulary," in a sense—of how relationships work. To do that, they were going to work with their partners to establish common definitions for the terms they used to describe their relationships together.

It's not hard to see why it's important to have common definitions of important terms within a couple. Imagine what might happen if everyone in Couples by Intention were talking about intimacy, but each person had a different sense of what it was! It would be like trying to talk about the color yellow. Close your eyes for a moment and imagine the color yellow, and try to think of an object that contains the yellow that you see in your mind's eye. If I were to ask that question of a roomful of 100 different people, there would probably be 100 different *shades* of yellow in what they reported back. Some might envision *lemon* yellow, some might see *golden* yellow, and some might describe *school bus* yellow. After a moment or two, it would become clear that we weren't all talking about the same thing when we use the word "yellow." We wouldn't be having a shared experience after all—even though before we closed our eyes and went through

> ▼
>
> **Imagine what might happen if everyone in Couples by Intention were talking about intimacy, but each person had a different sense of what it was!**
>
> ▲

the exercise, most of us would have *thought* we meant the same thing as everyone else. The word "intimacy" works the same way, which is why one of the first steps in becoming intentional as a couple is to build a simple, direct way of talking about intimacy so you begin to develop a common language together.

Intimacy: Our Definition

When our couple's group gathers, we establish a common definition of intimacy for us to use together. Here it is: intimacy is what we have when we can balance a sense of safety and vulnerability in a relationship such that they can both be present in equal measure.

Sit with that for a minute—the idea of balancing safety and vulnerability. An important implication of that definition is that if we are out of balance, with either too much safety or too much vulnerability, we cannot have intimacy. This is because if we are so safe we can't be vulnerable, we are guarded, defensive, and closed-off. But if we are so vulnerable we can't be safe, we're just terrified within the relationship. Intimacy is the important dance between the two so that there is neither terror nor inaccessibility between the partners. Safety and vulnerability have to balance each other out, "dancing" with each other, so that neither one has the advantage and both can flourish.

This dance of intimacy starts the very first time we meet someone new, and it changes in complexity over the course of the relationship. Let's look at how intimacy starts on a first date. Let's say that Daniel asks Seth for a date, he agrees, and they meet for coffee and are starting to get to know a little about each other. We'll sit with them through two scenarios, in two parallel universes, that each begin the exact same way. Let's watch as the two scenarios end very differently.

Daniel and Seth's First Coffee Date

Scenario 1

Daniel: So, Seth, what kind of food do you like?

Seth: I love Indian food! Never met a pakora I didn't like!

[Seth starts thinking excitedly that perhaps a next date could be Indian food!]

Daniel: Really? I hate the smell of curry!

Seth: Oh . . .

[To self: "Uh oh! Caution. . . . Daniel doesn't like what I like! We don't have that in common! Put your shield up!"]

Daniel: So . . . What kind of music do you like?

Seth: Um . . . [thinks for a moment] . . . I like all kinds of music . . . What kind do *you* like?

[To self: "Be careful! Don't let this be a second strike! Watch for potholes! Give a cautious and controlled answer!"]

Scenario 2

Daniel: So Seth, what kind of food do you like?

Seth: I love Indian food! Never met a pakora I didn't like!

[Seth starts thinking excitedly that perhaps a next date could be Indian food!]

Daniel: Really? I love Indian food! There's a great café downtown.

We should go sometime!

Seth: I would love that!

[To self: "Yay! He likes it, too! We have things in common! Open up and start investing . . . We've got a live one here!"]

Daniel: So, what kind of music do you like?

Seth: I know it's not that common, but I love Jamaican ska . . . It just makes me happy!

[To self: "Let's see what else we have in common!"]

The difference between the two scenarios is very simple, but it shows how safety and vulnerability start in the very earliest stages of connection.

Think about how Seth shifted in each scenario. In the first scenario, his hope of intimacy was squashed by disconnect, in part thanks to Daniel's responses. But in the second scenario, Seth felt more capable of balancing vulnerability (opening up) with safety (taking a calculated risk)—which is our definition of intimacy. This isn't to say that Daniel needed to agree with everything Seth preferred in order for Seth to feel safe, but the places where there *was* connection were powerful enough to help Seth feel safe enough to continue to self-disclose.

How could Daniel have responded in the first scenario such that he would have still allowed intimacy to grow, rather than stifling it? Let's revisit them one more time. In Scenario 3, you'll see that Daniel still doesn't agree with everything Seth likes, but he decides to be open, and to try showing his desire for Seth to be open, by asking him more about his experience. Let's take a look.

Scenario 3

Daniel: So Seth, what kind of food do you like?

Seth: I love Indian food! Never met a pakora I didn't like!

[Seth starts thinking excitedly that perhaps a next date could be Indian food!]

Daniel: Really? I have never really been a fan of Indian food. I find that my diet is a bit bland overall, though . . . maybe I should give it a try. Tell me more about why you like Indian food.

Seth: Well, I just really enjoy the adventurous feeling of eating something different than what I cook for myself. I feel like I get a sense of the bigger world when I branch out. If I don't like it, I don't finish it.

Did you see the difference? In this one, Seth got to be himself (he likes Indian food), and Daniel still got to be *him*self (he's never been a really huge fan of Indian food) but Daniel *invites* Seth to open up, and listens intently, showing a willingness to encounter Seth's uniqueness, even when—and perhaps especially when—it's different from his own. That's the power of balancing vulnerability and safety, and it's a good image of what intimacy can look like at its best.

Intimacy Is a Moving Target

Of course, the longer we're together and the more complicated our relationships become, the more complex it can get to balance safety and vulnerability! That's because the longer we're together, the more nuanced and subtle our communication can become. Because we are becoming more invested in the relationship, it's more likely that we'll try to avoid rocking the boat, as we begin to count on each other for more important facets of our life. Our futures, our desire to have children, our money, our deeper sexual and intimate desires—they all come into play. We have to be able to deepen our sense of safety with our partner as we engage in topics that are more meaningful than what cuisine we want for dinner!

Couples usually enter my office for the first time feeling disconnected, self-protective, and cautious. The road to couple's therapy often involves one partner dragging the other to the session, typically feeling that something or someone (guess who) needs to be fixed. The experience usually follows several attempts back at home to create change on their own without help. Here again, because we are never given a class on how to be in a relationship, we often try to connect in the best way we know how—but that might only mean that we use coping skills that make the disconnect even worse: avoidance, blame, strong reactivity, yelling, or shutting down. By the time they're in my office, couples may still feel some small flicker of hope, but there are battle scars and deep exhaustion between them. The goal of our work becomes looking to see where there is still "glue" in the relationship so that it can be extended and solidified.

John and Meili are wonderful examples of this complex dynamic. Prior to coming to couple's therapy, their arguing and fighting were persistent and increasing. Because John didn't like conflict, he would just shut down, coping with his negative feelings toward Meili (and toward himself) by playing video games, watching porn, and decreasing his overall activity. Because John had always been raised with the message that he was not living up to his potential, he developed a strong aversion to anything that would remind him that he was "less than," and he never developed the skill to name his feelings, speak his mind, or defend himself during conflict with a loved one.

Conversely, Meili would become more forceful and demanding, taking up the slack that John was giving her, simply because it was her nature to assume more and more responsibility when she saw an opportunity to do so. She became a whirling dervish as she took more and more duties upon herself, and she started demanding that John stop what he was doing, get involved, and stop being (as she saw it) lazy and disinterested. Things got worse when she found out about his porn usage; she assumed that he was no longer interested in her or the relationship, and she experienced feelings of hurt, rejection, and disrespect. Because she hadn't grown up with a solid relationship model, she assumed that John would just behave the way her younger siblings had when she'd bossed them around as the parent figure in their house.

The couples on my office couch are often afraid to talk in front of their partners, for fear of offending or hurting them or having to face repercussions for speaking their truth. There is a difference between "the" truth and "my" truth, because in relationships, there really is no one truth: each partner has their own perspective and understanding that needs to be respected. John and Meili were perfect examples of this principle at work. We spent our initial time together learning and practicing how to talk to each other *and* how to listen to each other as each shared their truth with the other.

One of the most important relationship lessons that John and Meili learned is that you can be right and you can lose—at the same time. Think about that for a moment: what does it matter if you're right if you are losing in your relationship? Both partners can be right—in their own truth—but the real goal is to do what is best for both of you and the relationship, not what will save your ego. Trying to convince your partner that you *are* right is a form of "helping," like we discussed in Chapter 1. It says, in effect, "I need to show you why you are wrong and what you should do about it."

The need to be right is often about a partner needing to solidify their own value in the relationship: if I am right, you will see that I am smart and that you need me to help you. If I am right, I can feel positive about myself and show strength. But what many partners don't realize is that they don't always need to be strong, and that they can be needed and valued without being right. Sometimes, being right is about needing the last word, in order to ensure that they have been heard. Being heard is often more important than being right, but when you don't know how to ask for confirmation that you have been understood, it's common to keep pushing your "right" perspective.

▼

But what many partners don't realize is that they don't always need to be strong, and that they can be needed and valued without being right.

▲

Spending time in therapy with both partners, defining what "winning" might look like for them, takes the responsibility and focus off of being "right." When we stop trying to be *right* all the time, we begin to see how we can *win* in our relationship, which only becomes possible when winning is negotiated and agreed upon by both partners.

But before we can begin negotiating what winning looks like, we have to have some kind of understanding of what we mean by "winning" in the first place.

Journal Questions

Intimacy Exercise 2—Right or Winning?

For this journal exercise, spend a few minutes thinking through these questions:

1. What is your definition of "winning" in your relationship?

2. What happens in your relationship when you try to prove that you are right?

3. Is it hard for you to let go of being right? Why? What would happen if you let your partner's truth coexist with yours? What would that look like?

Find the Link

Before couples can come to the group, we must work to reestablish their ability to identify the places where intimacy *does* exist between them, to name their challenges to creating intimacy, and to determine which skills need to be developed in order to close the gaps. John and Meili were a great example of a couple doing this work. I felt it was important that Meili's anger about John's porn usage be addressed prior to their participation in the group. Both John and Meili needed to feel secure in their connection so that their vulnerability wouldn't be exposed in front of the group in a way that could be demeaning or hurtful to either one of them. If they weren't able to trust each other, the group could potentially cause them undue distress by forcing them to face realities they didn't have the skills to handle well.

Bradley and Carol had to do some similar work to establish an intimacy-language, too. They came to my office hungry for connection and intimacy but unsure how to ask for it. Bradley was unable to shake the shame that he felt from growing up in a deeply religious household, limiting his ability to feel entitled to intimacy. He erred on the side of safety, because asking for what he wanted, or imagining what intimacy *could* look like between him and Carol, felt too raw and vulnerable. Somewhere along the way, he'd lost his voice.

Carol, on the other hand, was used to being in control. She had a strong voice and wasn't afraid to decide what would be done, by whom, and when—until it came to intimacy, in which case Carol completely lost her voice, just like Bradley. One common response I would get from Carol was, "I don't want to think about it. I'm doing everything for everybody, and I'm *tired*. I wish he would just know that things need to get done—and *do it!*"

Conceptually, Bradley and Carol understood there had to be a balance between safety and vulnerability, but they couldn't figure out how to make it happen. Furthermore, they didn't have a common language to talk about what would make them feel safe or vulnerable. They hoped their spouse would just *know* and take responsibility for providing it. We had several sessions together, as well as individual sessions, in which we focused on how to talk about intimacy. We spent a great deal of time learning a vocabulary for being intimate—how to talk about feelings, body parts, types of touch, and more. Learning to name and talk about feelings is an essential relationship tool.

Because we are never taught how to connect feeling to meaning, or meaning to words, most of us tend to be poor emotional communicators until we have help developing the communication skills to express what we want and to hear what our partner wants in words we can understand. Learning to speak our own truth about feelings, what they mean to us, and what we want others to know about them are an important part of developing intimacy together. (We'll talk more about this in Chapter 4.)

Use Your Words

In order to talk with each other about what you each feel and want, it's important to have a common language—a set of terms—that you can both use. So in my first session with a couple, I ask what language they use for their bodies and sex.

Most couples can't answer the question, and start to giggle or to look at the ceiling, or the floor, or anywhere but at me. Being able to name the body's parts, including our sexual parts, is the first step in getting to the emotional aspects of our bodies and what they mean for us. Yet few of us have ever been invited to talk explicitly about our body parts. I try to open the door for them to speak in this way. "It's all good," I'll say. "Honestly, we can talk like we are in a clinic, or we can talk like we are on a porn set—whatever works. I really don't care *how* we talk; I just want to use a language you are comfortable with."

This became particularly clear to me when I started working with Shira and Theresa, a lesbian couple.

Shira, Theresa, and Their Body Parts

Elliott: So, tell me: what language do you use when you talk about your body or how you use your body?

Shira: [After a prolonged pause.] We don't.

Elliott: So how do you tell your partner what is going on with your body or if you want something?

Shira: We don't.

Elliott: Okay. What is the name you give your genitals?

Theresa: [Giggling and answering in a whisper.] "Her."

Elliott: [Joining in the giggle.] Well, tell me about "Her"! Who is she? I would like to know more about Her! What parts make up Her?

Theresa: [Giggling, confused by the question.] You know— my "V."

Elliott: Ah, fantastic! And what about all the other parts? Are they friends of Hers?

Theresa: What other parts?

As it turned out, Shira and Theresa *did* have names for their body parts. Their vocabulary was already rich, erotic, and creative, but they had no idea that they were speaking in this language with each other already, when they thought they were just having fun!

Theirs was not a unique experience. One of the exercises I did with Bradley and Carol was to play what I call the "Name Game." I would name a body part or sensual act, and we would all take turns naming other words for that part or act. As long as none of the words got repeated, we kept going! For example: I would say "penis," and we would take turns with words like *dick, schlong, peter, cock, Johnson, pole,* and so on. Then the word might be *coitus,* and we'd name words like *screwing, fucking, humping, hooking up, banging,* and *thrusting*. When we'd run out of words, Carol would offer a new word, and we would play another round until it was Bradley's turn to lead. It was fun, and it brought lightness to a scary topic and allowed them to unpack their fear of language. The exercise also taught them that there are many ways of expressing what we want others to know about our bodies and how we experience them. The work can move quite quickly when it is facilitated and normalized by a therapist who can model comfort with language like this.

Journal Question

Sex Words

Stop here for a moment and respond to these questions in your journal.

- What words do you know that can describe sexual body parts or sexual acts? These can be words that you already use, words you've heard others use, or words that you'd *like* to use. (Examples: such as penis, vulva, vagina, "her," testicles, peter, cock, breasts, coitus, cunnilingus, etc.) Try to come up with as many as you can!
- What words do you like? Why?
- What words make you uncomfortable? Why?

Messages Matter

But it's not enough just to use words well with each other; it's also crucial to take careful stock of the messages we received about what being intimate should be like, as we discussed earlier in this chapter—and having a set of terms to use can help the process of naming the messages that we received. The strength in Bradley and Carol's marriage was clear: they had strong affection and respect for each other and a clear understanding that the other wanted to be in this marriage. Neither of them had any doubt about the other's level of commitment, and it gave them hope so that they were willing to do the hard work to make the marriage better. In couples like Bradley and Carol's, it's important to go back and look at the messages they received growing up about intimacy.

Look back to Intimacy Exercise 1 on page 53 and the messages you wrote down in your journal. How many of those messages did you summarily disregard when you got them? How many of those messages, positive or negative, are still with you today? How are they reinforced, either directly or subtly, as you try to change your perspective on what intimacy is and how it works? How have they affected the vocabulary you use when you talk about intimacy with your partner?

In the case of Bradley and Carol, the messages started in early childhood. Bradley was told by his parents and strong religious upbringing that bodies and sex were dirty and that they should never be getting any attention; paying attention to your libido meant that you were going down the road of perversion. Sex, Bradley's culture said, was only for reproduction within the confines of marriage, and any pleasure derived from it was self-indulgent. Carol, for her part, was never told anything at all. Her messaging came entirely from pop culture—movies, books, TV shows—and so she grew up believing that sex and intimacy simply *happened*. It wasn't positive or negative, so it wasn't something to look forward to or to desire particularly. Plus, because she didn't have a mother, there was no role model in her home as to what intimacy could look like between people who loved each other and wanted to go deeper together.

Sam and Yolanda received messages that were different from what Bradley and Carol got. Sam grew up with educators for parents. For them, talking about sex and bodies wasn't taboo. However, the comfort that his family has with sex and bodies set an expectation for Sam that men should be strong, vibrant lovers, ready to satisfy their partners when called upon. But Sam had a lower libido. So when Sam's personal experience didn't match the sex-positive messaging he received, he began to feel broken, as though something were wrong or deficient with him. Yolanda, as an only child, had been raised to be strong and opinionated, and it had been understood in her family that it was okay for her to advocate for herself. Yolanda's medical challenges also made her extremely aware of her body, and so the discordance between the positive messages she had about herself and the impact of her diagnosis, such as the side effects of medication and the challenges she faced in engaging sexually, often left her in a depressive state, torn between those two realities.

Yolanda's discordance also fed into Sam's confused messages about himself. He always looked to Yolanda to be the initiator and driver of their physical intimacy, and so when Yolanda wasn't in a space to drive sexual intimacy, Sam could capitalize on the distance in order to avoid doing any challenging work within himself that might help him better understand his sexual and intimate self.

With each of these couples, there had been decades of confusing messaging and reinforcement that needed to be rewritten when they walked in the door. Luckily, the work doesn't take decades when people are willing to question their beliefs; they can identify the roots of the messages they've received, and they have support for change.

▼

Luckily, the work doesn't take decades when people are willing to question their beliefs; they can identify the roots of the messages they've received, and they have support for change.

▲

A great deal of the work in the group is centered around ensuring that we are checking in on the intimacy balance, the dance between safety and vulnerability. When someone is being very cautious, I'll ask them, "What would allow you to be more vulnerable?" When someone is talking about or experiencing a high degree of vulnerability or caution, I might ask them, "What would make you feel more secure?" Often, the answer can be as simple as a confirmation that what is said in the group is truly confidential, or a show of hands that others feel the same way or experience the situation in the same way. As the group starts to form stronger bonds between the various couples, they will also ask this of each other and offer it up as personal insight. As a therapist, I've seen countless different situations and heard countless stories—and so there is very little in couple's personal histories or struggles that shocks me. As couples start to learn how normal it is to feel unusual, they start to become more comfortable opening up about the unique *versions* of unusual that they each carry with them—owning the uniqueness of their stories without shame, learning that they're not actually that scandalous after all.

The Power of Swagger

When thinking about intimacy, many people think of soft, quiet connectedness or perhaps physicality and touch. But when I think of intimacy and the balance between safety and vulnerability, I think of *swagger.* Swagger is important because it's the thing that helps us to cut across the challenges of the day to connect with our partner.

When I introduce the concept of "swagger" to couples, I get such a variety of reactions. Some people look like they just smelled bad tuna and make a face like I just said something offensive. Some give a questioning look because they've never heard the word and don't know what it means. Some even begin to panic, thinking that I am going to directly challenge their introversion and try to make them an extrovert!

What do you think of when you hear the word *swagger?* Most of the couples I work with describe it as confidence, presence, or some innate ability to pull someone's attention. Sometimes when we think of swagger, we have a comical stereotype of a hyper-dominant, hypermasculine male whose physical presentation has been carefully crafted to be larger than life, with an almost mythical quality that draws others to him. Think about Jay-Z or Mark Cuban. Some women might come to mind, too, like Anna Wintour or Beyoncé.

That's not the kind of swagger I'm talking about. The swagger I am talking about isn't grounded in the ability to be elite or to be above others. In fact, it's just the opposite: the ability to be confident enough to meet others where they are, to have the attention not just on oneself, but on others as well. In other words, to use swagger is to build one's connections and relationships without making it self-serving.

The role that swagger plays in creating intimacy cannot be overestimated, but first it's important to understand that *swagger isn't about you.* Typically, when our group members are asked how they would know when they had swagger, they respond with comments like these:

If I Had Swagger...

- ➤ I would feel confident
- ➤ people would respond to me with enthusiasm
- ➤ it would be apparent in my walk
- ➤ I could get people to acknowledge me
- ➤ people would be attracted to me
- ➤ people would listen to me

These responses presume that swagger is about *them* and how they draw attention from others. Remember, swagger is just the opposite: it's about the other person. Swagger isn't about how people respond to *you*, but how *you* respond to *other people*. It isn't about how others value you, but how you value others. It's about how you make others feel. Whether you are an extrovert or an introvert, it is not about going out and being the life of the party. It's about building connections one person at a time in deep and meaningful ways.

▼

Swagger is how you use your power and influence to engage others to create a deeper intimacy, because you have honed the ability to tap into vulnerability in a safe way.

▲

When you come home and your partner is happy to see you, you have swagger. When your partner has had a tough day and you can make them feel better, you have swagger. When your partner feels that you understand and value them, you have swagger. Swagger is how you use your power and influence to engage others to create a deeper intimacy, because you have honed the ability to tap into vulnerability in a safe way.

Another thing to understand is that swagger requires intention. It's not enough to fly on autopilot, the way we do with the day-to-day elements of our busy lives, letting things "happen" to us, if we want to have swagger. To truly exhibit swagger, we must show up to others, be present with them, and maintain the ability to have someone else's needs as our concern. People who are identified as having swagger are those who focus on others, those who make people around them feel special and important—all of which requires acting with intention, becoming aware of what their current feelings are, and what would make them change for the better.

Meili once shared something in our group session that spoke directly to John's developing swagger:

> **Meili:** When we first got together, John had no idea how hard my life was before I met him. He didn't grow up like I did. He didn't understand why I work the way I do or what I needed. I would get so frustrated with him. Over time, he began to pay attention. We had some hard conversations about what I wanted and needed and I really didn't like how he was responding. When we started couple's therapy, we would leave the sessions and not be able to talk. We got through it. Now, I find that I don't have to wonder if he is going to come home and notice me because he shows me that he gets me. We check in every day, and if he hears that I am having a rough day, he knows how to make me feel cared for. It really is what gets me through the times when I get frustrated with him!

Meili was addressing an important aspect of swagger. Many people think that either you have it or you don't, but in reality, swagger can be developed over time, and it looks different depending on who you are engaging with. John's response to Meili's comment exemplified this:

> **John:** Yeah, those conversations used to piss me off. I felt like everything I did was wrong and nothing would ever make her happy. I was like, "Why am I in this marriage?" What I learned in couple's therapy was that I was treating her the way I wanted to

be treated and not the way she wanted to be treated. It was so simple, but I had a brain explosion when I realized that if I just listened differently it would be so easy to bring the frustration levels down. I started coming home differently, and all of a sudden it was like I had a new wife. I mean, there are days that I just want to come home and not think about it because I am all up in my head, and those are the days that are tougher. Everything I knew about how to treat a partner had to change for Meili. What worked for me before wasn't working for me here. That was something I didn't realize.

What John was really talking about was that he needed to customize his ability to display swagger based on Meili's needs. A relationship with a different person would require a different approach. John's comment that "I was treating her the way I wanted to be treated and not the way she wanted to be treated" was hugely important, because it was the moment that John realized that to truly have swagger he had to make it about someone other than himself and be intentional about it.

Ultimately, that's why swagger matters. It's crucial for each partner to develop the confidence and self-assurance necessary to approach their partner, and the relationship itself, with a sense of purpose and deliberateness, or "intention," that considers the needs of the other person first. That's what swagger is all about—coming to understand the needs of your partner, and delivering on it with confidence and finesse over time.

Swagger doesn't mean, however, that we ignore our own needs or pretend that we don't have our own desires for the relationship. Actually, it's just the opposite: swagger, like we've said, requires intention—intention to be there for the other person—which requires that each person have a good understanding of what their *own* hopes and dreams are for the relationship.

It's a different angle on intention, but it's crucial for the relationship, so let's focus some attention on what intention can look like in a relationship.

Understanding Intention

I can think of few couples that better illustrate the idea of shared intention than Emilio and Mark. Here is a bit of their background as a couple.

Emilio and Mark

Emilio and Mark are a married gay couple who struggle to identify a common understanding of monogamy and sexual language. They both report that sex is great, but they don't know how to talk to each other about sex, what they want, and how it makes them feel. As a result, they have both gone outside of the marriage and have brought others in for sexual experimentation with each other. Whenever they try to talk about emotional or challenging topics, their discussions end as fights, each taking the other very literally, often responding with comments like, "But what you said was . . . "

Emilio and Mark have two children through adoption. Both men are committed, loving parents. Emilio was raised in a Catholic family that was strict but which had fairly progressive and accepting views on marriage and sexual orientation. He is close with his family and came out in college. After an initial period of challenging adjustment, his family has come to accept him and Mark as a couple. Emilio believes that "men should be men," and has narrow definitions of manhood. Prior to coming to therapy, Emilio never spent much time thinking about manhood as a concept.

Mark was raised in a fundamentalist church in which homosexuality was considered a sin and was demonized. Mark stayed closeted until well after college and never learned to talk about sex or his identity. When he came out as gay, he experimented heavily with sex until he met Emilio. He has no substantive relationship with his family of origin and holds Emilio as his foundation for family. Mark can be quite expressive and fluid in his presentation, but his deep sexual shame from growing up in a repressive environment causes Mark to question most of his decisions.

Emilio and Mark came to the group with a shared desire to broaden their intentionality beyond the sexual areas of their relationship into aspects of marital connection such as finances, parenting, faith, and more.

When couples start out on the Couples by Intention path, they set a course forward by learning what aspects of relationship they would like to explore *with intention.* Each couple and individual have their own area of exploration: Bradley and Carol wanted to explore intimacy; Emilio wanted to better understand his sexual and intimate language, and Mark wanted to create stronger pathways to feeling safe, and learn how to translate that security into his daily confidence. John wanted to find his voice, and Meili wanted to explore her curiosity.

Did you notice that? Emilio and Mark voiced *two distinct* hopes for their learning in the group. So did John and Meili. Understanding that each partner has their own personal goals is critical to the work. Not only must each couple understand their *joint* goals; each partner must understand their *own* goals, too. This need usually leads to a lively discussion on what intention means at an individual *and* a couple level within the group. A good knowledge of one's own goals in a relationship is the raw material for approaching one's partner and the relationship itself with purpose and swagger.

In one of the early sessions of Couples by Intention, I challenge the group to think about what happens when you do something on purpose.

➤ First, you must set a goal. It can be large or small, complicated or easy, but it all starts with some kind of goal to aim for. For example, one partner might have a simple goal like,

"I want us to make a habit of having ten uninterrupted minutes with each other right when we get home." Another partner might have a loftier goal, like: "I want to be able to draw better boundaries around our bedroom, so that our kids aren't in the room with us on Saturday mornings anymore, because that *could* be prime lovemaking time in our weekly rhythm." Whatever the goal, big or small, it's important that it be named and acknowledged.

➤ Once the goal is set, identify all the options around that goal, even the ones that might inhibit your ability to achieve it. In the example of the ten minutes at home, one option might be that the couple spends time on a park bench before walking in the doorway to start dinner; another option might be that they sit down with a glass of wine in the living room when they get home, and talk. In the bedroom example, one option might be to set a 100% off-limits rule with the kids (no more kids in the bedroom, period!)—and another option might be to have hours kids are and are not allowed inside. The options can be whatever the couple can imagine: the sky's the limit. It's just crucial that they be named.

➤ Next, evaluate each option on its merits, and value and rank them based on your desire and motivation to achieve them (first choice, second choice, etc.).

➤ Finally, you must actually select one option and decide to act on it. Give it a try and see how it goes!

In other words, intention requires *action*, and as you can see, the process of even deciding which action to take is a lot of work! What surprises many people is that it can happen in a short time or a long one; it can take place in a nanosecond, like when I make the decision to have my morning coffee, or it can take months, like when someone is thinking about proposing to their partner. It may also need to be a process that is repeated daily in order to achieve the goal. Think about going to the gym to achieve fitness, for example. The important lesson is that we are often intentional in our lives without even realizing the depth of the work we are doing!

Intention in Action: Making Choices

I often hear this question: how do intimacy and intention really work together? It all comes down to one word: *choice*. We make a choice—every day, seven days a week, 365 days a year—whether to stay in the relationship, or to leave it. So how and why do we make the choices we do?

Many people enter relationships with the assumption that we can promise each other forever—and in fact, many of us *do* make that promise—but that's not how connection works. When we strip away the happily-ever-after fantasies of eternal bliss and riding into the sunset together, we are faced with the reality of dirty dishes, unkind bosses, crying children, bills to be paid, and the other anticlimactic realities of our daily lives. So where's the magic?

It's in *choice*. You have the power to choose: stay or go.

Each day when you wake up and look at your partner, you make a choice that says, "today I choose you." Sometimes it may be, "I choose you because you are beautiful." Other times it may be, "I choose you because you are kind and take care of our family," or "I choose you because you work hard." But we also choose our partners *in spite of* their shortcomings: "I choose you when you ding the car." "I choose you when you need a shower." "I choose you as a *whole* person with all of your flaws and beauty." In essence, you're saying to your partner, "Today, I am in this. And in return, I need to feel chosen—chosen because I'm a good provider, chosen because I'm loved, chosen when I leave my dirty underwear on the floor, turned inside out, next to the hamper, chosen when I make you a surprise dinner, chosen because I am a whole person with flaws *and* beauty, chosen because *you* are in this, too."

Tomorrow, you will be faced with the same choice—but don't make tomorrow's choice until tomorrow. Just focus on right now, today. Be present. Be intentional. Allow yourself to be joyous, mad, frustrated, or excited. Whatever is going on right now in your relationship, choose to be in it when it is easy *and* when it is time to work. If you can't make that choice, it is time to leave.

Let's visit with Emilio and Mark again. In their struggles to grow together, sex was often "transactional" (about putting tab A into slot B) and not very relational (about the feelings and the relationship). The experience of transactional sex, aside from being less fulfilling, also opened them up to having others in their bed outside of their marriage and inviting others into their marital bed to be shared jointly. The problem with this was that they did not have an *intentional* agreement or make *intentional* choices with each other.

Emilio often commented that he was hurt. He said he was concerned that Mark was able to have sex with others and yet claim that he was still "in" the marriage and cared deeply about the sanctity of the union at the same time. Mark would reply that it was "just sex" and that he didn't see any issue with being with others as long as his heart and his deepest commitments stayed with Emilio. Getting the couple to identify what was really going on meant helping them to realize that the conflict wasn't just about sex—it was about being *chosen*. Emilio desperately wanted to be chosen by Mark, and he wanted evidence in their sex life; he wanted to be desired and to feel that he could meet Mark's sexual needs. Mark emotionally chose Emilio, but he separated sex from emotion after a life of living in the closet. Before Emilio and Mark could go any further in intimacy together, we had to identify why the situation was so challenging to both men, which allowed them to begin exploring the role and purpose of choice in their relationship. (We'll talk about various definitions of monogamy in Chapter 4.)

As a therapist, I get to witness some amazing things. I got to see John and Meili, who were struggling with connection and intimacy, begin to come together as they discovered how to balance vulnerability and safety. When they first arrived in my office, John would shut down when he felt disconnected, while Meili would become more forceful and demanding. Once they realized that intimacy didn't just happen, that they had to work at it, things shifted for them. John was able to develop his swagger and began to understand what would make Meili feel connected to him, and Meili could see what was shutting John down so that she could develop her swagger to invite him back to the marriage.

Sam and Yolanda, in the midst of their medical crises,

reported that while sex was more infrequent, they felt closer than ever and couldn't explain it. In reality what was happening is that each of them felt safer and were more vulnerable with each other as they supported each other through their realities. They also didn't focus on being right. They were focusing on what they each needed and what was in the best interest of the relationship in that moment.

Bradley and Carol, for their part, had to learn new language to begin to bridge the gap to intimacy. Even though they were smart and intelligent people, they were never given the communication skills and the actual words to connect. Today, Bradley and Carol are able to have what were previously challenging discussions about things they both were so hungry to connect about: sex and intimacy.

Wrapping Up

We've talked a lot in this chapter about the importance of being intentional in relationships. We began by looking at how dating apps have encouraged us to objectify each other like items at a grocery store, and how it's important to actually show up to one another as we're getting to know each other at first. We discussed the reality that the term "intimacy" has all kinds of meanings, and it's important to understand what you mean (and what your partner means) when you use that word. And we looked at how it's impossible to build a flourishing connection between you and your partner without deciding to be present, thinking of *their* needs first sometimes while still owning what *you* want, and having the confidence (swagger) to approach your partner with love and consideration.

As each of the couples we've mentioned in this chapter learned how to speak in the language of intimacy, they began to develop the basic tools necessary for any pursuit of deep connection between partners in a relationship. In Chapter 3, we'll dig a little deeper into what these tools can be used for, and how to use them to unpack even more assumptions that couples bring into how they relate to one another.

But first, let's do some reflection on Chapter 2.

Journal Questions

Chapter 2 Reflections

Now that you've finished Chapter 2, pull out your journal again and respond to these questions before moving on to the next chapter. Having read through Chapter 2:

1. What will you *keep doing* in your life and relationship that you are already doing?
2. What will you *start* doing, based on what you learned?
3. What will you *stop* doing?
4. What will you *think more about?*

Beware Assumptions!– Knowing Your Definitions and Role Models

In this chapter, you will:

- Take stock of any assumptions you might be making about relationships and gender roles

- Hear from couples as they unpack their own assumptions

- Learn about the power you have to change your assumptions

Remember Bradley from Chapter 1? He came to his first session alone, wanting to get to know me before he and Carol started their work as a couple.

His first session was focused on helping him share his story. He told me about his upbringing in a very religious family, and about his desire to be more connected to Carol, his kids, and his sobriety (he had struggled with alcoholism for much of his adult life). The session was going quite well and we seemed to have a connection— until I asked Bradley who it was that had taught him how to be in a relationship.

Dead silence. I asked Bradley who taught him to be a dad. Another long pause. "I was hoping you were going to teach me," he said.

Couples by Intention creates a container to explore the missing, confusing, and often unhelpful messages we've been given over the course of our lifetime about relationships, manhood, womanhood, intimacy, sex, and communication. As we move into the program, we start to take stock of the assumptions we've made about who we are and how we're "supposed" to relate to others.

Role Models: How We Come to Understand Relationships

Where did you get your definition of manhood or womanhood? Most of my clients have never stopped to think about where their definitions came from, or that other people might have different definitions than they do, so I often get puzzled looks when I ask. As we start to reflect on the root of these most personal of qualities, real stories that talk about how the relationship formed start to come to the surface.

Early on in Couples by Intention, I grab a large flip chart, write the word "Sources" at the top, and ask the group to name all the sources of information they can come up with of messages they've gotten about manhood and womanhood. (We talked about this a little bit in Chapter 1, during Intimacy Exercise 1 on 53.) The list usually includes things like these:

Sources: <u>Where</u> We Learned about Manhood and Womanhood:

> Family
> Faith
> Culture

➤ Friends
➤ Economy
➤ Television
➤ Social media
➤ The PTA
➤ Books
➤ Movies
➤ Porn
➤ The legal system
➤ The fashion industry
➤ Magazines
➤ Sports
➤ Education
➤ News
➤ Salaries
➤ The medical community
➤ Politics
➤ Racial stereotypes
➤ Stereotypes about immigration status
➤ Birth order
➤ Sexual identity
➤ Marketing

After that, I'll put up a second flip chart and ask them to start naming the *messages* they've received from those sources over the course of their lifetime. Usually, the responses go something like this:

Messages: What We Learned about Manhood and Womanhood

➤ Real men do; good girls don't
➤ Men are always horny but never needy

➤ Women are needy but never angry

➤ A woman's responsibility is to have children

➤ A man without a child is just a bachelor

➤ Women should own their own sexuality

➤ No means no

➤ No is confusing

➤ Even if a man is a caretaker, he must maintain his position as a strong person

➤ The shape of your body matters and determines your value

➤ The eldest daughter must marry first

➤ Birth order determines your responsibility/freedom

➤ Men don't apologize and women apologize too much

➤ Men are able to get erections at any time, keep it hard, and make it last for long periods of time, ejaculating large quantities

➤ Women get wet as soon as a man shows interest in her

➤ Men don't need to take extended paternity leave

➤ Women who take too much maternity leave are not committed to their careers

➤ Men don't show a lot of emotion, and if they do, they only show it to a few select people

➤ Women are overly emotional

➤ Men with low libido are uninterested; women with low libido are frigid

➤ Our parents insisted on monogamy, but open sexuality is what's expected in the culture now

As you look at the Sources and Messages lists, which comments resonate with you and the sources or messages you received in your own life? Which ones make you uncomfortable? And what do your responses suggest to you about your own story? Let's pause for a moment to give you a chance to journal some of your thoughts on

hese questions.
Journal Question

Messages

Time to break out the notebook again and think through some of these questions from your own life.

- Growing up, what messages were you given about your manhood/womanhood?
- Which messages do you agree with? Disagree with?
- How do you think these messages might show up in your relationship(s) now?

Diverse Stories

Making these lists always finds the group with very high energy, and conversation gets quite heated. The binary genders in the room are often amazed at the responses of the other half of the binary, and those off the binary have yet other responses. For example, when it comes to having children, women talk about the social pressure to reproduce. That they may not want to or may not be able to isn't mentioned to them, whereas men talk about feeling they had choices about whether or not to have children.

There are also different reactions across different generations: older members tend to give more traditional responses such as valuing monogamy over nonmonogamy, while Generation X, Generation Y, and Millennial couples tend to bring a broader blend of gender messages and sexual fluidity. But all of them tend to describe primarily *negative* messages, as in this exchange between Emilio and Bradley, which I think exemplifies the challenges for men:

Emilio: This has always been a very big struggle for me. Growing up in a Puerto Rican family, the message was always clear: "Protect your manhood at all times." In the beginning, it was confusing. Then it was scary because I knew I was different. Being gay and protecting my manhood seemed to be opposing messages. I spent years not knowing what to do. My father and uncles drank and screwed around all the time. I thought they were so fuckin' disrespectful. I wasn't gonna do that.

Bradley: I think I know what you are saying, only it was different for me. I am the son of a pastor. My dad had very strong messages on purity and chastity. Having sexual feelings was negative and bad. I learned that I should be ashamed of who I was at an early age. I wasn't ever told about sex and every time I tried to learn and got caught, it was really bad. By the time it came to dating and having relationships, I was always pulled between right and wrong, between what I wanted and shame. No wonder I couldn't get laid! Girls thought I was so awkward—because I was!

The women in the group are often quite shocked at the emotional challenges the men start to bring up. I remind them that in this aspect, women are far advanced, because the women's movement of the last 50 or so years has allowed women the chance to learn a language for talking about social and emotional oppression and the work that still needs to be done to fix it. Men are just now starting to develop a language that allows them to talk about the full range of their feelings and experiences, and in the group, the men often report feeling a tremendous sense of relief after a session when they see other men opening up about strong emotional conflicts. It begins to give the men a new way of seeing themselves.

Because couples are still in the stage of getting to know each other when we have the "messages" conversation, it helps to solidify the group's sense of community. Just the act of creating an environment where it's okay to name and process negative messages helps the group members to talk about how their relationships work and where the opportunities for growth might be. It develops for them a sense of curiosity that might not have existed before. "I always thought you were pushing against me for independence," said Sam to Yolanda in one of our group sessions. "I couldn't understand it, because I love that you stand on your own. Now I know that you are just fighting against all the crap your parents dished out to you!" Yolanda just smiled and said, "Yes!"

It's in hearing the stories of couples from other backgrounds and walks of life that we can come to realize messages we are carrying with us that we didn't even know were there, and the greater the diversity of the stories "speaking into" our relationships, the better we will be able to unpack the invisible messages that keep our relationships from reaching their potential.

Writing a New Story

Over the course of twelve weeks, we revisit this concept of "messages received" over and over. As we branch into other topics of discussion, members of the group will start to identify core messages that impact that discussion without any prompting from me. It's exciting to watch group members begin to challenge each other's past messages and check in a few weeks later to see how they might have changed over time. This has a direct connection to being in a relationship, where the point is to think and act intentionally rather than responding in whatever way has become status quo based on old messages!

Ethan and Valerie had plenty of experience being decisive in how they wanted their story to unfold, as you'll start to see when you learn a bit of their history as a couple.

Ethan and Valerie

Ethan and Valerie have been a couple for six years. They met in graduate school while each was going through significant transitions. Ethan was a transman who had just completed top surgery (mastectomy and reconstruction surgery to present in a more male form), and Valerie was coming to grips with the sexual abuse she had experienced in childhood. They came together through a shared need for safety, choosing to move in and live together shortly after meeting, which contributed to building a relationship that was deeply enmeshed and resulted in their losing their individuality. Plus, they worked for the same organization, had little divided time, and barely did anything separately. They were together just about all day, every day.

Ethan had identified as trans at age fourteen, and after some initial and difficult coming out, he received positive support from his family of origin. Because of his testosterone regimen, he passes as a biological male and wears facial hair. Ethan struggles to use his personal voice to ensure that his needs are met. He tends to be "of service" to Valerie even at the expense of his own desires, and so individual therapy for Ethan has focused on creating healthier boundaries with her. Ethan works as a teacher and loves his job, but he is often left feeling as though he isn't living up to his potential. He will often question whether he is doing enough with his life.

Valerie has received individual therapy for years, as she has learned how to process and live with her trauma history. Her relationships with her family of origin have been very challenging. As an only child, she never had to share a living space with anyone else until she entered her relationship with Ethan in adulthood. She is quite dependent on Ethan for many of her day-to-day activities, but she knows how to be the "director" of their relationship. She has strong opinions on social life and on how the household should be managed, and she has very high expectations of Ethan with no trouble speaking her mind to him.

Ethan and Valerie joined the Couples by Intention group because they were considering marriage and children. In couple's therapy, they had worked on creating better boundaries, and both had described their desires to model healthy relationships for their children. They planned to use a sperm donor, and for Valerie to carry the child. Their greatest hope from participating in the group was that they would reduce their enmeshment as they grew into more authentic individuals, strengthening their relationship by becoming two unique people in one relationship.

In many ways, Ethan and Valerie were already very experienced at writing a new story before they ever came to Couples by Intention: Ethan had been learning how to present himself more authentically to the world, and Valerie had been working to overcome the trauma she had experienced earlier in life, refusing to let it define her destiny. In both cases, they had refused to let "the way things were" lock them into a narrative that wasn't true to them.

Learning to determine and write a new story about life and relationships is an important part of the work that Couples by Intention participants do with each other, as we're about to see.

Writing a New Story, Example 1: Money

A great example of group members coming to understand the importance of writing their own new story comes from one of our sessions on managing money.

Meili: John and I have a common account. We put all of our money into the same pot and John does a great job ensuring that all the bills get paid. I trust him and know that he is doing all he can to make sure we are set for retirement.

John: I love that she trusts me so much, but sometimes I wonder how I got this job. It is like I am "the man" so I get the responsibility for money. It is a lot of pressure. The thought that I could screw it up freaks me out. We should both be responsible for it so that if the ship goes down, it isn't all on me! The other part of it is that I am always worried that I am never going to earn enough to pay for our life. Meili earns good money, but in her career, she is never going to earn what I do, so there is always pressure to earn, earn, earn. A man without a productive and lucrative job is like a woman without a baby. Because I am feeling bad about it I sometimes feel like I am hoarding my own happiness and can't be in the moment like I should and want to be. If I relax, everything is going to go to shit. I feel like it is like a Chinese finger puzzle where you put your index fingers in the ends of the paper tube and try to pull them apart. We have to come together to get out of that place.

Meili: I guess I'd never heard it that way before. Money confuses me. I get such anxiety about money. I grew up poor; we spent time living in a trailer. John's mother was a banker, and that made me feel even more incompetent about money. Talking to her makes me feel so damned stupid. Money is how we are seen. Sometimes my anxiety and insecurity about money makes me feel like I want to disappear. It is such a source of guilt and shame. I know how to earn it and how to be really tight with it. I don't care about who earns more, I really don't. But the whole system he has is just like "blah, blah, blah." I don't get his system and would rather not know all of the gory details. So, I guess I obsess over it and then ignore it when my anxiety and shame start to climb.

Carol: I certainly get that, but what happens if something tragic happens to John? I hope that doesn't happen, but what if? What happens to you?

Meili: I know. That scares me too, and then I put my head down and try not to think of it. I know I have to be better in this area but I just get overwhelmed.

After some more discussion between Meili and the group, it came out that Meili's father had also managed the money, and that Meili didn't have a mother, which meant that she didn't have a model in which both partners would have responsibility in this area. What Carol did was to challenge the definitions that Meili was holding and which had been set for her very early in childhood. By the end of the session, Meili had made a commitment to John to be more involved in the area of money management, and she agreed to have a meeting with a certified financial planner, much to John's delight.

That session of Couples by Intention also elicited yet another telling conversation about the power of money, this one from Ethan and Valerie.

Ethan: I get really concerned about saving for retirement. My father has worked hard his whole life and saved money, so I have been given models of what it looks like, but I don't own that. It always bothers me that I don't live up to that model. I am a teacher and I love to teach. But, let's be real, I am not making a ton of coin. I have real shame and guilt that I am not earning enough to help Valerie make other choices. Valerie has been after me to speak to a financial planner but I just dragged my feet, which really pissed her off. But I just felt like I was supposed to just know this stuff even though I don't. I felt like my manhood was in question. Again, I love what I do, but I am often thinking that I should just "man up" and quit my job and do something that pays more, so I can be "that guy." It took me almost eight months to call the financial planner and then another couple of months just to schedule the appointment. To be honest, looking back, I am glad I did it.

Valerie: I have to work so hard. I save what I can but we don't talk about money. I think planning is everything. I need Ethan to be able to talk to me but when we talk about money he often just emotionally disappears.

Ethan and Valerie's story showed the group how strongly a couple's finances can affect the power dynamics in their relationship. Managing finances, regardless of what model and approach is used, has to include both partners. Money is one of those critical issues that form the foundation for safety, security, flexibility, and power dynamics. Having both partners take part in the process ensures checks and balances and safety. Much as Carol pointed out in her question to Meili ("What happens if something tragic happens to John?") each partner needs to be able to jump in and take care of the family, even if the other one is the de facto money manager. In Meili's case, she needs to know what resources the family has, where they are located, how to access them, and what is owed against them. If Meili can't jump in at this level, the risk to the family is great.

It's important to be curious about the role-modeling and messages we receive in childhood so we can become more intentional in our approach to many things, including money, with our partners. Many couples describe the triggering effect that money and finances can have in the relationship. In fact, next to sex and intimacy, financial issues are among the most frequent topics that couples will go into denial about. How much someone earns, the potential for earning, the money put aside for retirement, what inheritance or family money is being brought into the relationship, and any history of poor money management or bankruptcy, can all lead to feeling inadequate, unbalanced, or other uncomfortable emotions, so people just want to ignore the whole conversation because it's just too hard. This is so clear in Meili's response to Carol's question: "I know: that scares me too, and then I put my head down and try not to think of it." Being intentional about facing the emotional and tactical challenges of money management may require the help of a professional financial planner, and there is no reason for shame in that! Sometimes we have to look outside the relationship for help from an expert.

Writing a New Story, Example 2: Parenting

As conversation about role models and messages develops from week to week, couples in the group eventually come to the topic of children and parenting. More than during any other session, this is the week when inherited messages about manhood, womanhood, and relationships rise to the surface, and a lot of our attention is focused around one simple question: "Which of these messages do you want to pass onto your children?"

▼

"Which of these messages do you want to pass onto your children?"

▲

As the conversation starts, I remind the group that children learn much more from what we do than from what we say. The subtle messages that are embedded in our behavior have a significant impact on how children make sense of the world, so it's very important that we examine our messages, so that we know what we're giving our kids.

Actually, the initial discussion starts even before that, with the question of whether or not the goal is even to have children. Couples in the group tend to have very strong feelings on this issue, though they're not usually well articulated yet. Two conversations on the topic of children show how dramatic the impact of messaging can be upon this crucial aspect of building a relationship together. Let's turn to Emilio and Mark again.

Emilio: I always knew I wanted to have children. I never thought that being gay meant I couldn't have kids, but I never knew how it would happen. Coming out to my family wasn't easy, but it was certainly easier than telling them that I wanted to have children.

Mark: When we first got together, it was one of the things that most attracted me to Emilio. He has such a strong commitment to family and family values. It felt safe to me. However, I struggled. I grew up in this very fundamentalist family that told me over and over again that homosexuality was a sin and that to bring children up in a house of sin would be unforgivable. I got the message loud and clear. I was a sinner, and children would never be a part of my future. Meeting Emilio started to change how I thought of all of that.

Emilio: Yeah, I think that was one of the hardest things in our relationship—balancing what we wanted for our future and the guilt and shame that our families tried to put on us. Many of our friends didn't get it, either. Either they had similar messages like we got or they were gay and couldn't imagine how having kids would work. They assumed that we would need to bring in a lot of help, meaning women, to help us raise the kids. When we told them that we were not using a nanny but that we would be able to have flexible schedules and we would take care of the children, it was equally confusing for them. It was like no matter who we talked to, we couldn't get anyone to see it like we did.

Mark: We felt very alone. Once we started moving forward, we realized that we only had each other to rely on. Slowly, some people came around to being supportive, but several of our family members still struggle with us and with the family we are trying to raise.

Emilio and Mark were really able to talk about the messages they received about manhood, parenthood, and gender roles, along with their struggle to make sense of it all. Whether or not to have children was clearly a decision that would define them as couple, and they were seeing that it was a decision that needed to be made with great intention and with curiosity as to *why* they were doing it.

Sam and Yolanda clearly understood the importance of the conversation, too, because they had experienced these things first-hand themselves. Even as an unmarried couple, they had been exploring their fertility options due to Yolanda's challenging health. For her, it had been a long and frustrating road of trying to unpack messages with the men she had been close to over the years.

Yolanda: I was very open with Sam from the beginning. I didn't want any surprises. With past boyfriends, when I talked about my health with them, they either ran for the hills because I was "broken" or they stayed with me because they thought I was "safe" and that they could have sex without unwanted consequences. It was really frustrating. When I was younger, I wasn't very good at determining what the dynamic was. With Sam, it was different. I told him about my health and he just said, "Okay, so let's figure out what that means." It was foreign and cool at the same time to be with someone who wasn't so black-and-white about it.

Sam: Don't think I was some super-chill guy. I wasn't. It was scary. I want to have children. I love kids. But I also know that there are lots of ways to have kids. Look at Mark and Emilio—two kids, right?

Yolanda: [Giggling.] Yeah, I guess we're kind of in a similar boat as you guys. You're "sinners" and we're "broken"! I'm not sure which one is more challenging. [No longer giggling.] As all of my girlfriends started getting married and having kids, the pressure got to be too much. Everyone kept asking me when I was getting married and having kids. I began to hate going to weddings and baby showers. I kept feeling the intense judgment. The fact that I can't just "get pregnant" is so painful for me. I don't have any siblings to have kids that will make my parents into grandparents. My parents think that being grandparents is a critical part of their future, so they put all this pressure on me—and they know my medical status. I am supposed to be responsible for their happiness. It's as though if I don't bear children, I am less of a woman. I get so pissed off.

These two conversations exemplify the often difficult messages that couples find that they've received from the world around them. In Emilio and Mark's case, the not-so-subtle message was that two men can't raise a child. Emilio and Mark were very open about their frustration at being met with comments like, "Must be Mom's night off!" or, "How nice that Dad babysits." (In those situations, Mark is quick to clarify that "Dads don't babysit; they parent.") The assumption that there must be a mother for the child to be doing so well, or that Mom taught Dad how to be a parent, is deeply disturbing to Emilio and Mark, and they've taken to being very protective of their children. They want their kids to have a counter-message to use when they hear negative messages about having two dads. Emilio and Mark want their kids to know that men *can* parent and love, and they *can* provide everything a child needs.

In Sam and Yolanda's case, the message exemplifies a misogynistic, contradictory view of women. On the one hand, women are told to be strong, with messages like, "Don't take a back seat," "Be equal to men and demand equal pay for equal work," and, "There is nothing a man can do that a woman can't do." But on the other hand: "If you don't want to have children, there is something wrong with you," and "If you can't get pregnant, you're broken." In other words, women are told that they can do everything men can do, but they still tend to be valued on the functionality and use of their uteruses.

Listening to these messages, and hearing experiences of some group members, other members were quick to offer their own stories of what parenting means and the messages they had been given. The men spoke of the expectation that they should get their wives pregnant; women supported Yolanda's story and shared their own experiences regarding pressure, having to balance mothering and work, and how being a mother often came at the cost of a meaningful career. The stories just poured out, one after another.

▼

It's the first time they've come to realize how much power they have for changing themselves and how they live their relationships.

▲

Every time I run a new Couples by Intention group, this particular week is always pivotal, as participants hear stories from their own partners they had never heard before. In this, the gender dynamic shifts several times during the night: men align with men, women align with women; men are stunned, women are shocked. In an era when gender roles and expectations are changing, couples begin to learn that they can craft their journey intentionally, regardless of how it aligns with messages they grew up with. They get to shape their messages themselves if they want to, and for many of them, it's the first time they've come to realize how much power they have for changing themselves and how they live their relationships.

The Power to Change

Whether the group is talking about money or parenting, each couple is able to identify and share how they are impacted by the role models that were put in front of them and the social messages they have been challenged to accept blindly. Partners are encouraged to use their power to demystify, change, and counter those messages, and as they begin to learn how, the group's energy increases.

Emilio and Mark went home after talking about how they rallied against negative messages to build their family. Success! John and Meili and Ethan and Valerie were all able to face their fears and denial about money and how to talk about it so they could make their financial health a part of their relationship health. Success! Sam and Yolanda were able to talk about facing the reality of infertility in the face of social expectations and find strength in each other and from the group. Success! There was growth everywhere, and now the group members were able not only to describe what they meant by the use of the word "intimacy," but to begin crafting it in a way that made sense for *them*, regardless of what the rest of society thought. It was a powerful time.

Wrapping Up

But it didn't end there: it never does. This chapter has walked you through the important steps of thinking through messages you have received about relationships and gender-roles, and the power you have to re-write your story for the future. It's important now to understand how to use those tools to describe what the *boundaries* of your relationship should be. In Chapter 4 we'll do some more eavesdropping on group sessions as couples explore what they mean by the word "monogamy."

But first, as always, let's pause and reflect.

Journal Questions

Chapter 3 Reflections

Now that you've finished Chapter 3, pull out your journal again and respond to these questions before moving on to the next chapter. Having read through Chapter 3:

1. What will you *keep doing* in your life and relationship that you are already doing?
2. What will you *start doing,* based on what you learned?
3. What will you *stop* doing?
4. What will you think more about?

4

Monogamy, Monogamish, and Nonmonogamy

In this chapter, you will:

- Discover that the term "monogamy" refers to more than just sex

- Explore the "Monogamy Scales"—the areas of life, outside of sex, where partners can feel betrayed

- Learn how to set boundaries about what's okay and what's not okay between you and your partner

Remember the guy from the Introduction who couldn't understand how his relationship got so "fucked up"? His name was Chris. When he first came to my office, he told me the story of how he and his wife got into a pattern of not talking, not having sex, and defaulting to a relationship that was basically that of friends or roommates, not partners. "I just thought that's what happened in a marriage," said Chris. "After a while you just become good friends and you get laid once in a while if you're lucky."

But what Chris didn't account for was that his wife was having a deeply emotional relationship with a co-worker named James.

Chris was dumbfounded when he found out, feeling betrayed, frustrated, and utterly at his wits' end. "How could she have all these feelings for a guy at work and not be able to do that with me?" he wondered in session. Chris and his wife had agreed to have a monogamous relationship, he said, but while Chris reported that he was pretty sure his wife never had sex with her co-worker, the damage to their intimate connection was done, and Chris' feeling of being transgressed bigtime was complete.

Monogamy Is Monogamy . . . Or Is It?

What Chris didn't yet know was that monogamy is one of the most misunderstood aspects of being in a couple. From childhood, most of us are presented with strong, unyielding messages about monogamy, and we assume that *our* definition of monogamy is *the* definition. We are told that the princess marries Prince Charming and they live happily ever after. We read stories and watch movies where the main characters are destined for each other and only each other. Relationship betrayal is held up as a lack of character in our social norms. We get these messages and we either hold dear to them or rebel against them. Do we hold onto the relationship when things are tough, and prove that we can withstand the pain? Do we actively shed society's norms because no one gets to tell us what the right thing is for us? Do we blindly accept monogamy as a rule because it represents normalcy and safety?

▼

Monogamy is one of the most misunderstood aspects of being in a couple.

▲

Whatever your concept of monogamy, it's important to be sure that you understand where your thinking comes from, and *it's essential that you choose your monogamy state intentionally.*

Most people identify monogamy in terms of whether or not they're allowed to have sex or sexual contact outside of the relationship, but such a definition is confusing at best. For example: what *level* of intimate touch is allowable, and what would cross the line? Would it be okay to hug someone else? Would it be okay to give a friend a back-rub at a party if it were in front of other friends? What if it were in private? If a back-rub is okay, how about a lower body massage? If that's okay, where do you draw the line?

And it's not just about touch. One of John's sexual practices was to look at pornography online. He particularly liked looking at chat rooms because the performers were live and he could chat and directly engage with them in real-time. He told Meili that he never paid any money for the service and always used it as an unregistered, anonymous user, never sharing any personal information with the performers. But the interaction was purely erotic, even if it was a thrill without any commitment. Online, he could be anyone he wanted to be, telling the performers any story he desired. From his perspective, it was all about *him*, and he didn't have to be concerned with whether the performer achieved any satisfactory state. John reported that he enjoyed this experience because he was able to achieve a gratifying orgasm through masturbation, and he could be his erotic self without feeling judged or shamed by the performer, the way he often felt around Meili.

Meili, however, had a very different perspective on the situation. To her, what John was doing was an infidelity—an online affair, a sexual experience with a different person—and she felt very angry and hurt. But that only confused John, as evidenced by his response. "How can this be an affair?" he asked. "I haven't touched anyone but myself! I've never even been in the same room with her! I don't know her name! She's in another state! She never saw me and doesn't even know what I look like! How is this any different from if I were watching a porn movie, looking at a magazine, or reading erotica?" Meili struggled to answer, and eventually replied that "It is! It just is!"

When Monogamy Isn't Defined

What makes a conversation like John and Meili's so painful is that both partners want to have their sexual needs understood and met, and they are struggling to figure out how to communicate that that's what they want, all of which is getting lost amid the issue of the chat room. John's insistence that he hasn't had a relationship with anyone else is his attempt to say, "I don't *choose* anyone else."

Meili's response, pointing to John's diverted energy and attention, speaks to *her* desire to be the focus of *John's* desire.

A related challenge showed up with Emilio and Mark, because their definition of monogamy was more "monogamish" than monogamous. Both partners had had outside sexual partners, and there was a fluidity to how they expressed themselves sexually. When they first started working in my office, I asked them whether monogamy was their goal. They hesitated, struggling with the answer, but finally Emilio spoke up. "I suspect the right answer should be 'Yes,'" he said, "but I'm not sure. Our sex life together is great. We get together and magic happens. Sometimes we just want to bring a different type of excitement to our bedroom." Mark agreed. He spoke of how their individual one-offs weren't about sex or connection or intimacy, but more about stress relief and decompressing from life's challenges. Just having sex made him feel more relaxed, and he didn't want to talk or process after the fact. In other words, for Emilio and Mark, monogamy meant something other than simply "keeping it in your pants."

The type of struggle that these two couples were facing made me start to think of monogamy in a new way. Couples kept asking me for a more concrete way of thinking through monogamy other than intangible, value-based conversations that left everyone feeling judged by society and held accountable to a ritualistic standard that had been summarily handed to them by the world they grew up in.

So I did what I do in most sessions: I went to my whiteboard and started to write down examples of what it was that everyone was talking about when they used the word *monogamy*. This is how I developed what I call the "Monogamy Scales," a way to break down the elements of monogamy and allow couples to see what assumptions they had built into how they used that word.

Monogamy Scales

Here are the elements of monogamy that I've compiled through ten years of couple's therapy, showing the areas of life in which the greatest sense of discord takes place in most relationships. These items are broad strokes, but they've been useful for me in helping couples to take the idea of monogamy out of their pants, applying it to the *whole* self instead of just to the genitals. The Monogamy Scales are composed of these things:

- ➤ Sex
- ➤ Physical touch (nonsexual)
- ➤ Emotional connection
- ➤ Intimacy
- ➤ Social interactions
- ➤ Familial connections
- ➤ Financial security
- ➤ Spirituality
- ➤ Politics

Let's take a look at each of these areas. *Sex* is the area of life where the erotic side of someone's being is located, whether we're talking about genitals, hands, mouth, or other body parts—any experience that can be considered erotic. These experiences can be with oneself, with another person, or with multiple others, and they might include masturbation, dancing in an erotic manner, intercourse, or oral sex, among other things. When I ask couples how they define *sex*, I hear a variety of answers, usually having to do with aspects of nudity, penetration, orgasm, ejaculation, or erotic body contact, but the truth is that a simple touch can be erotic even when it's nothing even remotely like coitus. For example, if someone kisses you on the cheek, it usually means "Hello! I care about you!" If someone kisses you on your jawline, the message is slightly different, as it seems more erotic. When the kiss lands on your neck, there is a significantly erotic tone. Three kisses, three different messages and levels of intensity—all across a space less than three inches across!

Several times, couples have expressed to me that one partner experienced a particular kind of touch as erotic even though the other partner had not, like when one person says something like, "I don't like the way she touched you at the party. Her hands were all over you." Clothes may not have been ruffled, there might have been no bodily fluids exchanged, and the encounter may even have been right there in public, and yet it can still look and feel like a sexual experience. That's why when we're talking in the realm of *sex*, it's important to understand that we're not just talking about penetration. Any touch at all can be sexual.

Nonsexual physical touch has to do with respecting that we each have different needs for personal space. It is not uncommon to have partners who have very different comfort zones when it comes to touch, such as when we think about the ways we say hello and goodbye to friends and family. One partner might hug and kiss everyone, while the other might offer a more formal handshake. One partner might give a full-body hug, while the other offers an "A-frame" hug, making sure there is as little physical contact as possible. It all depends on a person's language of nonsexual physical touch.

As humans, to be touched is one of our core needs. In fact, babies who are never touched fail to thrive. These babies begin to lose weight, lose their appetite, become easily fatigued, and have delayed development, among other things. Being touched by people we love and feel secure with can be an extraordinarily healing experience for whatever ails us, and it can be deeply personal without having to be erotic. Many of my patients will offer me a hug at the end of a session, simply because they and I have experienced some kind of intimate, personal, nonsexual connection during our session together, and it can help to re-center them as they head out into the world. More often than not, it is my heterosexual male clients who open for a hug because they are the people least likely to be given safe touch in their day-to-day lives. Anytime we're dealing with touch that's not intended or interpreted to be erotic, we're talking about nonsexual physical touch.

Nonsexual physical touch is critical between partners. The ability to cuddle on the couch, give a quick nonsexual kiss goodbye on the way to work, or hold hands while walking on the beach can be a shared moment that centers and confirms our place in the relationship and our ability to trust the bond that has developed. Often this touch is described as *more* desirable than erotic sexual touch when a partner is feeling disconnected, lonely, or challenged.

103

Emotional connection focuses on our ability to experience, name, and share feelings. These include all of the joy and happiness that we experience, as well as more challenging and confusing feelings like anger, frustration, and sadness.

Understanding what expressions of emotion mean is just as important as being able to experience them. Sam reported that he felt like Yolanda was angry all the time, which made him feel sad and insecure. "She yells and is always upset about the stupidest things," he said once.

"I am *not* angry!" she replied. "I'm *Italian*! It's how we talk!"

That little moment of clarity helped Sam to see that an expression of affect may or may not constitute a deep feeling, like how in Yolanda's culture, talking loudly did not necessarily mean someone was angry; it was just a way of talking. Sam learned that he needed to be more curious about what was going on for Yolanda and not to assume that he knew her feelings just by the way she talked.

Some partners are more able to easily process an emotion openly and feel comfortable with emotion, while others process their emotions more internally and with limited expression. That's not to say that one partner is necessarily "better" at emotion than the other; it's just a difference in processing, an alternate way of using emotion to connect. However we process our feelings, our ability to share, communicate, and understand each other emotionally creates a foundation for building a good understanding of monogamy together.

Intimacy, as we've discussed, is the balance between safety and vulnerability, and it's a balance that we share in all of our relationships, not just in our coupledom. Friendships, parent-child relationships, workplace relationships, and other forms of bonding all contain some element of intimacy, and so it's important that you and your partner have an understanding of what *levels* and *expressions* of intimacy are appropriate if they involve people other than your partner. For example: what information can and cannot be shared outside the coupledom? Can you talk about your sex life with your friends? Can you share the intimate details of your marriage with family members? What is private and what is public? Couples need to discuss these things together.

The rules don't have to be consistent throughout the relationship. For example, Emilio didn't feel the need to have a great deal of intimate sharing outside of his relationship with Mark. Because Mark frequently wanted to process feelings and intimacies with Emilio by talking about them together, Emilio felt as though he didn't have any need to share any intimacies from the marriage with anyone else. "It isn't anyone else's business to know what is going on in my marriage," Emilio said. "That's private." But Mark sees it differently; he needs to find validation from others, and he doesn't have the same familial support that Emilio has, so he doesn't get the generosity of family members' pouring support into the relationship. Mark's friends *are* his family.

Emilio said that he understood, and that he wasn't threatened by Mark's need for conversation with others. "If he wants to go do his 'girlfriend' chats, what do I care?" he said once. "In fact, it kinda helps me because then he only brings to me the things I need to know. I don't think I need know everything, and we have an agreement that if I say, 'This stays private,' it will."

As John and Mark showed, partners may have varying needs for connection in relation to each other, and so it's important that they come to agreements about what can and cannot be shared outside the relationship. Any time we're discussing dynamics like these, we're dealing with intimacy.

Social interactions have to do with how individuals and couples interact with friends and acquaintances, and how those interactions affect the sanctity of the relationship. Some couples lead very separate social lives with unique groups of friends, rarely bringing the other when they spend time with their circles, perhaps because one partner has very little need for social events while the other has a strong social need, or because one person spends a significantly greater amount of time working than the other. Whatever the reason, these couples do not share social supports, and each gets by just fine on their own.

On the other end of the spectrum, there are some couples who are completely enmeshed, never to be seen apart. They work together, they socialize together, they do everything together, perhaps using the "Yours, Mine, and Ours Rule" for social support: *your* friends are *my* friends are *our* friends.

Ethan and Valerie did everything together. They rode to work together. They worked in adjacent buildings for the same company, so they were able to have lunch together every day. They rode home from work together each night. In fact, other than during actual work tasks, they were almost never apart. Valerie had talked about wanting a "girls' night out," and Ethan said he supported it, but Valerie never made it happen. When asked why, she said, "I don't know. It just feels like I'm doing something wrong." For Ethan's part, he readily admitted that he enjoyed her company. "I really like it when she's here and it's just us," he said. "We get each other and it's easy." Ethan and Valerie knew when they came to couple's therapy that talking about their social interactions was going to be a big deal.

Alternatively, Sam and Yolanda had very active and unique social lives. Sam was a writer and was often out with his writing collective working on stories. Yolanda was an artist and was often in her shared studio space with her artist friends. One of their common discussions centered around trying to find time to do things together, both with and without others.

Sam and Yolanda could celebrate their unique circles of friends. Their challenge was to learn how and when to carve out time to socialize by themselves, and when to blend in their different friend-groups so that their relationship could be stronger.

Familial interactions can bring a great deal of support for a couple, or cause a great deal of distress. How couples decide to involve, relate to, and connect with family members presents another dimension of defining monogamy in their relationship. Do they always spend the holidays with one family or the other, or do they try to balance them out? Do they call their in-laws "Mr." and "Mrs.," or by their first names, or by "Mom" and "Dad," or by nothing at all? Do they see their families as two separate entities that are each connected to one of the partners, or are the families blended into one large web of support that holds them up as a couple?

This part of connection can become painful when one partner has a close and intimate relationship with their family of origin and the other partner either has no family or has a negative connection with theirs. This was the case for Emilio and Mark. Emilio had a large, loving family, who welcomed the couple and their children at every opportunity and were actively involved in the couple's life. By contrast, Mark had no relationship with his family of origin, a fact that caused him great distress, and his reaction was to hang very tightly onto his in-laws to try to fill the gap that his own family had left. In fact, Emilio often joked about the difference in their approaches to family. "Sometimes I think Mark is with me so he and my mother can have a relationship," Emilio said once. "He talks to her much more than I do." Because Emilio loved his family but didn't have strong skills or desire for deep, shared intimacy outside of his marriage, Mark could support Emilio's familial connections by being the more involved partner. Emilio loved his family, but he found the energy required to maintain strong connections challenging, and so they agreed that Mark could be the bridge between the couple and Emilio's family in a way that Emilio appreciated and that fed Mark's need for family connection.

Sam and Yolanda had a different experience with family. Due to their known and documented infertility challenges, their parents were keenly aware of the medical interventions they were planning for having children. Sam's parents kept a respectful distance and didn't ask too many questions. They took an approach that essentially waited for Sam to tell them what he thought they needed to know. For many reasons, Yolanda's parents, in particular her mother, were always calling trying to get every bit of information. She wanted to know when Yolanda ovulated and when she was taking medication. She even asked about Sam's sperm count! Sam and Yolanda spent a lot of time in therapy discussing where the boundaries with family should be in this part of their life. To do this, they had to agree what was and was not allowed to be shared outside of the marriage, and with whom.

Financial security and money issues are among the most challenging topics a couple must contend with. Disclosing one's financial health to a partner can raise deep emotions from fear, shame, blame, and belittlement because they are afraid of being judged by their partner as incompetent, irresponsible, or underperforming. (Many couples, in fact, come to my office simply to have this discussion.) But even though such conversations can arouse feelings of vulnerability, they're a crucial part of building an understanding of monogamy together.

Bradley and Carol had to conquer this milestone early in their work. Bradley tended to be financially conservative, having developed a nest egg over years of frugal savings; Carol loved shopping and had large amounts of student loan debt. When they first came together, Carol was hesitant to tell Bradley what her financial picture looked like, because she knew that Bradley understood how to manage money and was good it, and that she wasn't as strong in that area. Carol would shop to manage her emotions: she'd shop from being happy, shop from being upset, shop from being bored. It was completely unlike the way that Bradley managed money, and she knew it. "If I really share with you what the numbers are, I know you will be angry," she told Bradley in session once, "and I just don't want to have that fight."

"Well," replied Bradley, "if I don't know, I assume the worst, and I feel like I'm the only one that cares about our future. All I see are new leather boots, and bills."

How to manage money and determining the *meaning* of money are often difficult, no matter how much we earn. How do you set financial goals and meet financial challenges? Do you share everything, or do you keep separate accounts? Do you split the bills and expenditures fifty-fifty, or do you settle on a percentage? Setting about trying to decide how enmeshed a couple's finances can and should be will often uncover deep feelings of personal self-worth and identity along the way, as Bradley and Carol showed in their struggle as to how to even raise the subject of money in the first place.

Very few of us are trained and talented when it comes to financial management when we enter into a relationship, but I find that couples are typically able to make significant growth and find a greater depth of understanding in this area. Often, one partner will be the financial manager in the family, and the other partner will know little or nothing about how the money is being managed and what plan is in place for the future. Whenever this particular session comes up in Couples by Intention, several group members will become visibly tense. When they open up, they describe feeling "stupid" or "childish" because conversations around money make them feel overwhelmed, or they don't understand financial matters or are afraid to take on the responsibility and risk financial ruin. Having walked through these things with couples for many years, I've learned always to recommend that couples have a monthly financial meeting to talk about financial planning. That conversation every few weeks helps to ensure that both partners can understand the plan they've developed together and to know where the resources are, even if one partner continues to be the financial manager. I also recommend that the couples speak to a certified financial planner in order to educate themselves on how to make good financial decisions based on their values, dreams, and future goals.

Spirituality, for some couples, refers to the idea of a higher power, religion, church, and childhood teachings. These couples often enter a relationship asking, "Must I marry someone of the same faith background? What happens if I don't?"

But for many couples, spirituality means something completely different. I ask about spirituality with a question I often use to get at the deep meaning of something: "So what?" This question has to do with what something *means*. For example: "My partner watches a lot of porn." I say, "So, what does that mean?" Asking the question that way moves the conversation beyond the reasons (such as, "He watches porn because it helps him to masturbate") and into the meaning that the action conveys (such as, "It makes me feel like our sex life doesn't have enough excitement because he is looking for something new").

Spirituality also has to do with how we honor the sanctity of the union, such as with the use of rituals and special traditions, which can create a sense of ceremony in the relationship. For example, a couple might say, "We only go to the café on our anniversary or other special moments for us. We never go to the café just for dinner, nor do we ever bring our friends there; it's our special place that has deep significance for us."

Any time a couple is dealing with a higher power, or with meaning, or with ritual, they are working in the realm of spirituality.

Political monogamy has to do with the ideology of each member of the couple. Can a Republican marry a Democrat? Is it necessary that both partners share a strong ideological perspective on the world, or can they connect if they see the world through differing lenses? I've seen couples break up over the inability to share a value-driven understanding of the world, and I've also seen couples whose different ways of viewing the world became a very strong form of attraction between them, challenging each other to grow and think differently. Sam had ended his previous relationship because he and his ex-partner didn't see the world and their future through a shared lens. But on the other hand, remember Shira and Theresa, the lesbian couples that had challenges naming their body parts? Their main attraction to each other were their stark differences. Shira came from a highly political, conservative, Israeli family while Theresa came from a nonpolitical, left-leaning family. They were initially attracted to each other precisely *because of* their political differences, because they enjoyed being challenged to stretch and see the world differently. The point is that anytime we're dealing with people's ideological leanings and the way they affect the relationship, we are dealing with the *political* element of being a couple.

Monogamy Is Complex

As you've seen through this discussion of nine different dimensions of monogamy, the term *monogamy* itself, like any relationship, is never cut-and-dried. Each of these areas has the power to make us feel either balanced between safety and vulnerability or challenged to become more connected to our partner. These dimensions all operate on a spectrum from monogamous (a closed and unified system) to consensually non-monogamous (an open system that allows others in). For the couples that I work with, including the ones in Couples by Intention, much of the work becomes focused on increasing each person's curiosity about the other, so that they can better understand each other and create more meaningful connections between them. Being able to put the pieces together into a larger narrative that describes the other person not only helps each person to get to know the other better. It also helps the couple to talk about monogamy with the same understanding as to what that word even means. (See Figure 1 for an illustration of all of the scales in one place.)

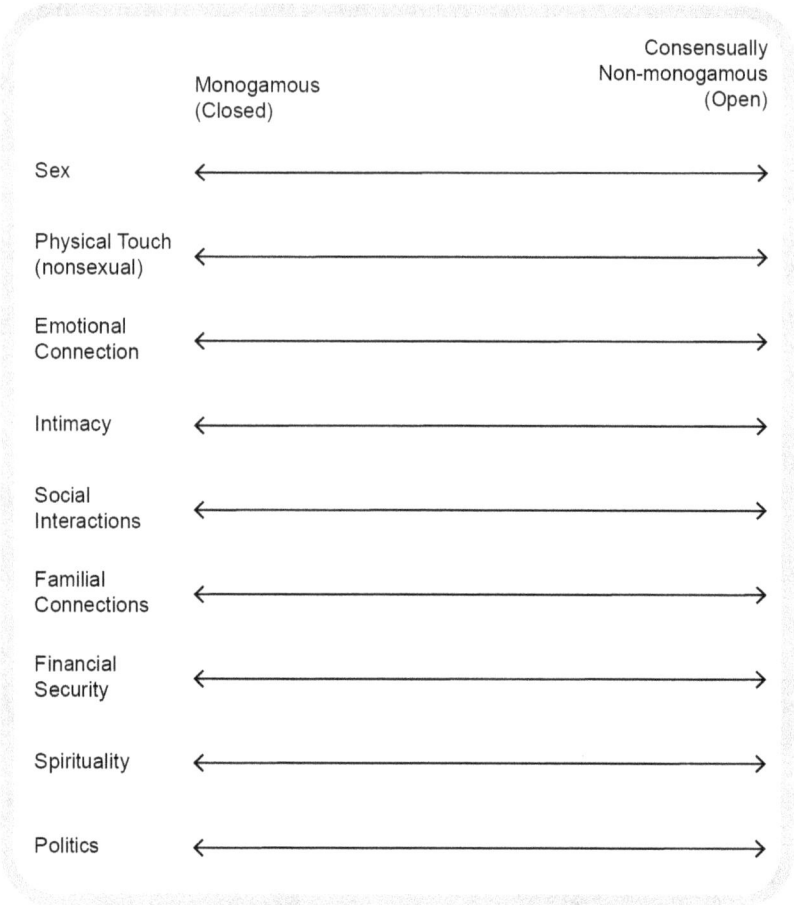

Figure 1: Monogamy Scales

In session, I draw these monogamy scales on my whiteboard. After explaining the different dimensions of monogamy and hosting a conversation about mindfully withholding judgment regarding the appropriateness or "rightness" of each other's perspectives, I give each partner a marker and ask them each to think about and identify where they would place themselves on the scales in each area, somewhere between completely closed (monogamous) and completely open (consensually non-monogamous). A tool such as this helps partners to express themselves visually as a way to start a conversation together as a couple about what they want monogamy to look like for them.

Let's look at Sam and Yolanda. The two of them initially came to my office because Yolanda's medical conditions were challenging the couple. Both partners were focusing on what it would take to have children and how Yolanda's medical conditions were affecting her ability to work and to have great sex. Sam wanted to be supportive, but he wasn't sure how. He described Yolanda as beautiful and sexy, but they weren't having much sex. Yolanda wanted Sam to initiate more, and she described their sex life as "pulling teeth" or "deciding to take care of it myself." Meanwhile, Sam felt pressured to "man up," and he felt left out of the sexual experience. From his point of view, he didn't think that Yolanda even liked their sex life, so she was having one without him. Yolanda and Sam loved each other and were committed to making the relationship last, but there was clearly more going on than just Yolanda's medical diagnosis.

I asked Sam and Yolanda to mark themselves on the monogamy scales. Figure 2 shows how their diagram looked.

Studying their diagrams together, Sam and Yolanda started to realize that they were similar in their understanding of nonsexual physical touch, emotional connection, financial security, spirituality, and politics. It only took a quick discussion around those items for both partners to feel that they had attained a common understanding of monogamy in those areas.

In the areas of sex, intimacy, social interactions, and familial connections, however, Sam and Yolanda were further apart, which suggested that they were going to need more exploration.

As the two of them started telling their stories about these broader differences, some themes began to emerge. They found that their sexual encounters were gratifying to each of them, and while they desired more touch and sexual experiences with each other, they didn't feel that the concern was great enough to risk any damage to their happiness. Yolanda enjoyed masturbation and was happy to have Sam watch, and Sam reported that simply knowing that that was true relieved him of the insecurity that he was underperforming. Sam operated under the assumption that all sex in their relationship had to involve both of them, and that because she wanted more than he did, he was failing. Yolanda placed her mark closer to the center of

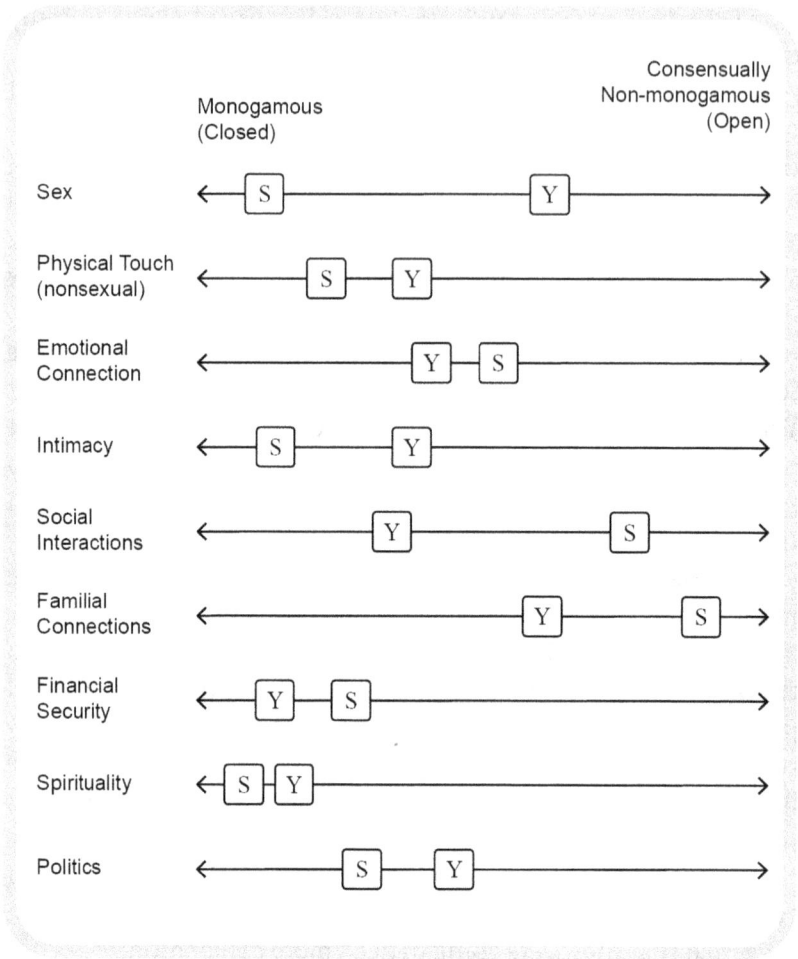

Figure 2: Sam and Yolanda's Monogamy Scales

the scale not because she desired to have sex *with anyone else,* but simply because of her desire to have sex with *more than just Sam.* She wanted her sex life to include masturbation and self-exploration. Because of their discomfort in talking about sex, their conversation might not have happened as easily if they hadn't used the scales.

Sam and Yolanda's different views on social interaction came to light through the scales, too. Yolanda, with her broad connections, extroverted personality, and large circle of friends, felt that she got a great deal of her intimate conversations from her girlfriends. Sam, who was more introverted, felt relieved to learn that he could be himself without the need to go out and socialize like Yolanda did. Additionally, knowing that his introversion didn't cause Yolanda to feel disconnected allowed him to remain present with her without worrying that he wasn't meeting all of her emotional and social needs. Yolanda confirmed Sam by explaining that she wouldn't share information that would be sensitive or private to their relationship. To help Sam feel more comfortable, Yolanda promised that if she was unsure whether something could be shared, she would ask Sam what he thought; Sam would be sure to tell Yolanda if there was something that he definitively wanted to make sure was private. Once Sam began to relax more, his anxiety dropped and he began initiating sexual contact more.

The other sources of stress had to do with their family connections. Sam had come from a close-knit family that had given him a strong foundation for what a connected relationship should look like. His parents modeled intimacy and closeness and had always shown their children that it was okay to be playful with one's mate. He described his relationship with his family as connected but a bit distant because they lived out of state. Yolanda, as an only child of immigrants, felt deeply enmeshed with her own family and wanted to experience the same thing with Sam's side even more than Sam himself did. Being able to talk through how they presented themselves as a couple allowed Sam to give Yolanda more freedom to connect to his family because he didn't have to own the role of bridge-builder anymore, and over a few months of stepping back from that position, Sam reported that he felt more comfortable with his own family because Yolanda had become the link between the couple and Sam's side. Before using the scales, that kind of arrangement might never have occurred to them, or might not have felt okay if it had.

Emilio and Mark used the scales to discover where they were struggling, which allowed the men to identify what the real foundations of their marriage were. What they learned was that it wasn't the sexual nature of the extramarital experiences both men had that created a sense of threat, because it turned out that both

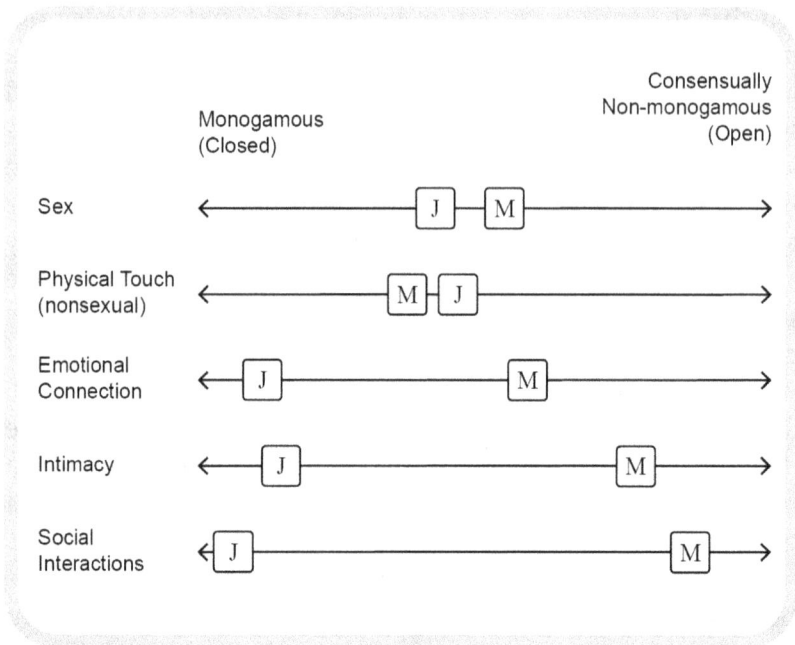

Figure 3: Mark and Emilio's Monogamy Scales

men were quite comfortable and confident with sexual touch with others, both together and apart. Mark was confused about how Emilio could be comfortable inviting others into their bed and occasionally having individual experiences, but sometimes he was not okay with Mark's sexual activity. Emilio would be triggered anytime Mark would talk about those experiences in a familiar manner or if there were repeat experiences with the same person. The key scales for this concern in their relationship are listed in Figure 3.

By looking at the scales together, Emilio and Mark were able to determine that the primary source of Emilio's concern was that he had a need for a more closed system when it came to how they expressed intimacy and emotion and how they socialized. Mark was far more comfortable sharing his emotions and intimacy across a broader social spectrum. Mark felt no concern talking about the narratives he had for his sex life, his marriage, or personal life experiences with others. His sharing took place with a variety of audiences including lovers, friends, and members of Emilio's family. Looking at the scales allowed Emilio and Mark to begin negotiating new, healthier boundaries for their relationship, making space for each partner's needs. Once they realized that their conflict wasn't actually about the sex but about emotion and intimacy, rooted in Emilio's feeling threatened by Mark's disclosures, there was a tremendous shift in how the two men worked together in the relationship. Emilio was finally able to tell Mark that it was the emotional and intimacy infidelity that hurt him, not the sexual experience itself.

Couples trying to overcome infidelity are often surprised to discover that the greatest injury between them isn't really the *sexual* infidelity—but *elements in the other scales instead*. Having learned these varying dimensions of monogamy, the partner who feels betrayed is able to express the pain with nuance that they might not have had before, and the partner who committed the infidelity is able to describe the pain that led to it more accurately.

▼

Couples trying to overcome infidelity are often surprised to discover that the greatest injury between them isn't really the *sexual* infidelity—but *elements in the other scales instead.*

▲

Bradley and Carol had to work through Bradley's infidelity as they were going through couple's therapy prior to joining the Couples by Intention group. Having worked with the monogamy scales early in their time with me, Carol came to discover that her greatest need for healing was in the areas of intimacy and physical touch. While she could understand and forgive Bradley's addiction and how it drove Bradley to act out in inappropriate ways that were damaging to the relationship, she continued struggling to let him become close to her. It became apparent to both of them that Carol was focused not on the specific infidelity that Bradley had committed with his penis, but the infidelity he had committed with his hands. "I hate his wedding ring," Carol finally brought herself to say. "I need him to get rid of it. Those hands, that ring, touched another woman. How can those hands ever hold me safely again? How can that ring mean anything anymore?"

After much work healing the deep wounds that came with Bradley's infidelity, Bradley and Carol became friends again, enjoying each other's company and feeling positive about the future—but even after months of work, they weren't touching each other. It was time to address the issue of touch directly.

Around that time, Bradley said that he felt ready to engage in intimacy with Carol again, but Carol balked. "I know how sorry he is," she said in session one morning. "I believe him. He has worked so hard to address everything. I know we will be okay, but I just can't get over his hands. It's his hands! I want him to have new hands!"

Carol's disclosure of her feelings toward Bradley's hands led us to ask how we might work creatively toward helping her perceive them differently. Because Carol was a faithful Catholic, we discussed going to a church so that Bradley could wash his hands in holy water and receive a blessing on Bradley's hands. Carol wasn't sure that that would be enough. "I have this image of his hands touching," she said, and so our strategy shifted: Carol needed a secondary image of Bradley's hands to counter the one she was carrying in her mind.

> **Elliott:** Carol, what if we could get you another image, one of Bradley's hands doing something that aligned with your values? Would that help you see his hands differently?
>
> **Carol:** I don't know. Maybe. But what could that be?
>
> **Elliott:** Let's think about it. You love to cook.
>
> **Carol:** [After a thoughtful pause.] We could knead dough.
>
> **Elliott:** I love that idea. That would also put you in control. The teacher. The mentor. He would learn from you.
>
> **Carol:** What if it was pasta dough? Then we could form all the pieces of pasta individually.
>
> **Elliott:** Then you would be able to see his hands doing several different activities!
>
> **Carol:** Yes! We could make pasta puttanesca! Pasta street-

walker style! Then we could eat it! Oh wait! Then we would shit out the waste!

Elliott: Yes! Literally getting rid of the bad, unwanted part of what he made with his hands!

Carol: I love this! Yes! Bradley, will you do this with me?

Bradley: Yes! I would do anything that helps you feel better. Yes!

Carol and Bradley had struggled for so long to be able to identify the chasm in their connection, and simply identifying a new link between the two of them—through something as simple as pasta, of all things—allowed them to be more open to what could be! Addressing the nonsexual breach of trust and faithfulness was the road back to connection.

Setting What's Okay and What's Not

The scales also help couples to identify the boundaries around the relationship and to determine the rules that the couple will use for interacting with the outside world, whether it's with parents, with children, with work, with friends, or with people who flirt with one partner or the other. When couples come to me for help negotiating what a consensually non-monogamous relationship could look like, I ask them to tell me how clear they are about what they are hoping to achieve. Usually, they think that having an open relationship is easier than a monogamous one, but once I explain the scales, they come to realize that even though a strictly monogamous relationship is the clearest, it's not necessarily the easiest or the most appropriate for them. A strictly monogamous relationship—in which there is *no* touch whatsoever outside the couple, *no*

▼

Relationships work best when each individual is allowed to experience the world uniquely and bring their learning, growth, and understanding back to the union.

▲

outside socializing, *no* individual savings or spending, *no* difference in political viewpoints or social ideology between the two partners—would be deeply enmeshed, unhealthy, and unrealistic.

Rather, relationships work best when each individual is allowed to experience the world uniquely and bring their learning, growth, and understanding back to the union. The more non-monogamous a relationship is, the more negotiating, expectation-setting, and communication there must be. The key is to discuss, agree upon, and understand whatever levels of consensual non-monogamy are best for that particular relationship, so as to ensure a deep trust between the partners and an ability to reconvene and share. Couples may decide that certain scales require absolute monogamy while others can be more open, like when a couple decides to have strict financial monogamy but to have an open non-monogamy in how they socialize with friends. I am always telling couples that *the healthiest relationships have the clearest boundaries.*

The scales teach couples how to frame their connection as a whole-relationship version of monogamy, rather than only focusing on *sexual* monogamy, which can create a relationship as unique as its partners, such as the world has never seen.

Wrapping Up

Of course, simply defining the outer bounds of the relationship is only one step, because contained within those negotiated lines of monogamy is the real content of the relationship itself—a whole universe to explore and unpack together over time. In this chapter, we've talked about how the term "monogamy" is actually much more complex than couples ever thought, and impacts relationships in ways that are invisible until we think about them carefully—for example, in terms of friendships, money, politics, and spirituality. To delve more deeply into the space between partners, which is the heart of the relationship, we'll need to talk about how to engage each other and stay interested in one another for the long haul. Let's turn there in Chapter 5—right after you take stock of what you learned in this chapter.

Journal Questions

Chapter 4 Reflections

Having read Chapter 4, haul out your journal again and spend a little time responding to these questions. After reading Chapter 4:

1. What will you *keep doing* in your life and relationship that you are already doing?

2. What will you *start* doing, based on what you learned?

3. What will you *stop* doing?

4. What will you *think more about*?

What's Better Than Sex?– The Power of Curiosity

In this chapter, you will:

- Learn about the essential power of *curiosity* in your relationships
- Gain some skills in how to listen a*ctively w*ith your partner (and show it!)
- Explore the "four buckets" of emotions—and *how* easy it is to confuse one emotion for another

Whenever I'm at a party and people hear that I am a sex therapist, I quickly become the center of conversation as people ask about all the crazy things that they imagine I talk about in my office. They expect me to tell them about clients with wild sexual experiences, strange dysfunctions, and scandalous revelations, anything that will titillate them, because they don't get to talk about sex and intimacy as openly as I do. Many of them aren't even aware of *how* to talk about those things, even though they very much want to.

But when people become overly curious about my work, my sense is that they're judging themselves against any potential story I may share. Like the couples in my group, they want to know

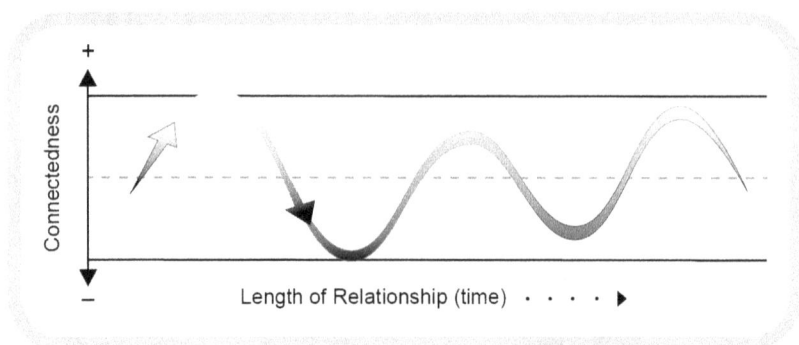

Figure 4: The Relationship Wave

where their relationship sits on the spectrum of "successful" versus "dysfunctional." In short, they want to be validated.

So when the little crowd has gathered around, I'll often ask them a question that tends to stump people: "Do you know what keeps a relationship together more than love and sex?" Now I've got their attention, and I can see the hunger in their eyes. They want the secret. Better than love and sex? What could it possibly be? Aren't the primary components of a happy marriage love and sex?

Before I cue you into how I answer that question for the party-goers, let's take stock of some facts about how relationships work. Anyone who has been with another person long-term can tell you that love and sex have peaks and valleys, periods of high and periods of low. If it's true that love and sex create connectedness, many relationships would resemble a sine wave, like in Figure 4.

When couples are at the top of the pattern, they want to hold it for as long as they can, because being at the top of the pattern feels safe, fun, and work-free. At the bottom of the pattern are seasons of concern, despair, anxiety, and we find disconnectedness and risk. We tend to want to get out of those spots as quickly as possible.

The Wave Can Be Disorienting

Each couple's "wave" pattern looks different, but there are a few trends that have generally held true for couples I've treated. For example: some couples get caught in a "low" part of the cycle, find that they don't know how to get out, and begin to become anxious or frustrated or to despair.

Meili was particularly eloquent during one of our group sessions when she opened up about her own "low" period. "I get so frustrated," she said in session once, "because I get caught in my own head. I know that John just thinks I am being rigid or trying to punish him. But I'm not! I just don't know how to get back to the good place—you know, where everything is okay again!"

The rest of the group sat completely enraptured as Meili told her story. Hers wasn't a unique experience; other group members had experienced their own valleys on the sine wave of connectedness with their partners, and they wanted to know how they could climb back up to the top and breathe the fresh air of closeness again. And so I begin to instruct them about the single-most-important element of closeness, starting with the same answer that I give my party friends: *curiosity—the ability to keep learning about one's partner in new ways over time.*

The Power of Curiosity

The closest, most intimate couples have learned not to assume that they know everything they need to know about their partners. They still allow their partners to influence them and the way they think, which can be a tremendous opportunity for growth. Curiosity allows each partner to listen to the other one differently, in new ways, eager to uncover new layers of how their partner thinks, how they encounter the world. Being curious allows for the reality that one's partner may have information that can be key for one's deeper understanding, growth, and awareness. Curious partners show that they are paying attention to each other and are willing to verbalize their thoughts, questions, and feelings as pathways to learning something new about the other person.

Anyone can develop curiosity. It's like a muscle: it needs to be stretched, worked out, and built up over time, and the more it gets used, the stronger it becomes. Nobody masters yoga in a single session, and no one learns the art of medicine in five minutes. The same is true with developing curiosity about one's partner.

It can be intimidating and scary to build curiosity. At the beginning of relationships, curiosity seems to come easily. We've just met someone new and we want to know everything we can about them, and we want to tell others so that they can feel good about the connection along with us.

But after we've gotten some basics and surface-level information, our curiosity about the other person starts to diminish. Once we know that the other person is interested in a relationship, we begin to shift from curiosity to assumption. We start to assume that we know what the other person thinks and feels, which gives us a false sense of connectedness. We might think, "I know you so well that I know what you think and feel, and it makes me safer."

▼

The more intimate we become with another person, the more challenging it is to know them, because the deeper down we go, the more unique they and we are!

▲

In reality, the more intimate we become with another person, the more challenging it is to know them, because the deeper down we go, the more unique they and we are! The fear of not knowing our partner at this level can often leave us feeling that our relationship is not as secure as we imagine. A well-developed sense of curiosity about the other person, especially at those deep levels of familiarity, strengthens our relationships, because it ensures that we are connecting truthfully and openly.

As we develop curiosity, it's important that our partner knows that we are being intentional about it, that we are present and paying attention to them. If we are doing it effectively, it will also communicate to our partner that we need them to be intentional by working just as hard at being curious as well.

Even if we are effective workplace or social communicators, intimate communication is a different skillset. In the workplace, the communication tends to center around service, leadership, and goal attainment. In social settings, communication is based on building connections while keeping strong boundaries. Intimate communication takes on all of those aspects and more. It requires a deeper commitment to another person than other forms of communication, and the stakes are higher and the risks more apparent. In the workplace and in many social situations, expectations are often clear, even in writing, as to how we are to behave and communicate, but in our intimate relationships, we have to craft the rules in a way that's as unique as the person we are committed to.

"I get so frustrated," said Meili one night at Couples by Intention, "because John has all these friends at work and he is funny—like, *really* funny. They love him. It's like, as soon as we're around those people at a work event, John lights up and so does everyone else. I don't understand why he doesn't bring that same guy home with him."

Others in the group said they knew just what Meili was talking about, having seen that their partners could communicate more easily in some situations but had a hard time communicating within the relationship.

"It isn't that I like my coworkers more," John replied. "I hate my job and my boss is a jerk. I have a shared experience with my coworkers and we have private jokes to help us get through the day. But when I'm at home, I'm not giving them any of my time or thought. I don't need to cope with work when I'm at home, and I don't want to talk about it anymore when I'm home. I want to forget about all of that. So when Meili keeps asking me about my day, it's like I have to talk about crap that I don't want to Meili and I don't need to share that, so I would rather not. Why doesn't she ask me about me and not my day? No one at work asks me about me."

Sam and Yolanda had similar struggles with communication. "There are some days I just don't want to share," Sam said in session one night. "I am bored. I worked. I came home. It was the same as yesterday. I am out of work and I don't want to talk about it anymore. I mean, when I talk about it, I bore the hell out of myself! And yet, I constantly get, 'How was your day? Tell me about it! What did you do?' Ugh. That's the worst part of coming home—having to talk about my day!

"I wasn't taught to talk," Sam went on. "My parents didn't talk, and maybe I'm just repeating patterns of how my family was. My mother was a homemaker and did a great job. My dad would come home around 6:30 and we would run up yelling, 'Yay! Dad's home!' We would eat dinner and not talk, usually with the television on, and then we would all go do our own thing—and wash, rinse, repeat the next day. But Yolanda has this ability to turn a six-hour work day into a 17-hour story! She tells every nuance, every detail—'... and then Gloria sneezed ...' Sometimes I don't know if I can survive another let-me-tell-you-about-my-day story."

"He's right," Yolanda agreed, laughing. "I like stories. I want to talk. I want to hear. We have been apart all day. I'm craving reconnection! What I'm learning slowly, sometimes very slowly, is that if I can be quiet, I can get more. It isn't my nature to do that. I am trying not to ask, 'How was your day?' because that question usually doesn't get me anything that I need. I am starting to ask questions like, 'What was the one best part of your day?' and 'What is the thing that you put the most energy into today?' When I ask questions like that, Sam is more likely to give me something that has meaning for me, and he knows that it isn't going to be a run-on conversation. We both get to win!"

Meili smiled and chimed in. "Yes! I just made a big connection," she said. "I am such an external processor, and John is such an internal processer. When I try to process the day externally, John just gets annoyed because I am forcing him to do what he isn't good at and doesn't want to do! But I can't stand the silence. I struggle with it. It is so awkward to be so silent with someone that I am supposed to be so connected to. What you helped me to understand is that the silence isn't rejection of me but rejection of the processing! This is what we need to work on!" John smiled and nodded.

The Sweet Spot: Not Too Much, Not Too Little

Language and communication start when we are babies blowing bubbles and raspberries. That's when we learn to use our lips, tongue, palate, and throat to make sound. Eventually we move on to simple words, simple sentences, and spelling, which evolve into basic paragraphs in school, which turn into full-blown essays. Most people are trained in each one of those levels, whether through family or through school. But we're basically on our own

```
Too much: Snobbish/talking down/arrogance
─────────────────────────────────────────
The Sweet Spot: Opportunity for meaning
─────────────────────────────────────────
Too little: Childish/unskilled/incapable
```

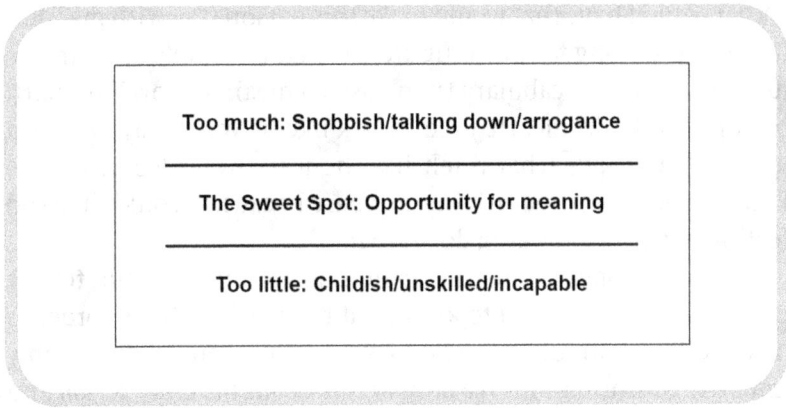

Figure 5: Layers of Communication: How We're Perceived

to figure out how to communicate intimately. We might take our cues from TV, our parents, friends, books, and other sources, but there are no courses to take on how to communicate in intimacy, so most of us enter our relationships ill-equipped to manage the complex system of intimate communication.

In all communication, especially intimate communication, there is only a narrow stratum of opportunity where we can communicate with any kind of effectiveness. If we communicate "below" that space, using undeveloped thoughts and language, people think we're stupid and ignorant, that we don't get it. But if we communicate "over" that space, using overly complicated language and concepts that are needlessly abstract, people think we're snobs. They think that we consider ourselves better than everyone else, as though they're being talked down to. We have to find the "sweet spot" between those two extremes to communicate effectively, and we have to adjust the location of that space with every single person we engage (see Figure 5). If we don't hit the spot just right, communication starts to degrade.

Valerie shared with the group the lessons that she learned from her relationship prior to getting involved with Ethan. She described her former partner, Brian, as highly educated, having come from an academically driven family. Valerie first met Brian when Brian was working in higher education. "When we first met," said Valerie, "I was amazed that someone so smart was interested in me. I thought,

'What could I have that would make this person stay with me?' But it didn't take long for me to figure out that he wasn't so smart: he just had a better vocabulary than I used. I mean, I know I'm smart, but I just talk like me. He used to talk like he was always giving a lecture, and that's what it felt like: he was always lecturing me. Pretty soon, it started driving us apart because I couldn't stand feeling like he was talking down to me."

Some people think that communication is about telling people things they need to know, but the truth is that in order to be effective communicators, we have to go a step beyond simply imparting information. *We have to care about the other person* and whether or not they've actually comprehended the message we're trying to send them. In relationships, we usually communicate in order to gratify ourselves, not our partner. For example: let's suppose that when I become angry, I tend to yell. I may know that my being loud and forceful shuts you down and closes you off, but I need to expel the heat that I feel inside, and I expect you to receive it. When I do this, though, I am communicating to gratify myself, not you, and you will have received nothing but conflict and defensiveness. But if I'm angry and can tell you I'm angry in a tone and language that you can understand and accept without being put on the defensive, you are more likely to want to help me, and you might even respond to say that you understand that I'm angry, without becoming closed off.

Another way we communicate to gratify ourselves happens when we get "lost in the message"—that is, not stopping to *consider the context of how our partner is likely to receive what we're trying to express*. In Chapter 1, I mentioned that my partner sometimes puts my coffee cup in the dishwasher before I am done with it. If I just say, "Please don't touch my coffee cup," one might think that that is enough information, because it is (to me) clear, concise, and direct. But my coffee cup often *does* end up in the dishwasher, and it happens for a reason. If I take a moment to think of *why* my partner might move my coffee cup to the dishwasher, I realize that there are lots of possible explanations: perhaps because he is just trying to be helpful or he wanted to clean the kitchen. Perhaps it's because he has anxiety about having an unkempt house and can't tolerate the mess. Now, it's true that I'm interested in the backstory, and because I care for his feelings, what I really need to communicate is, "Please don't put my cup away as I am not done with it yet, but *I promise that when I am finished drinking coffee, the cup will end up in the dishwasher.*" That would be a more complete message, and it may invite a better response, because it addresses and affirms whatever reason my partner has for moving my cup. Generating greater clarity between one partner and the other often requires us to increase our amount of communication.

Another key is to *be careful not to take what you hear literally.* Couples can often be heard saying to each other, "But what you *said* was . . . " which indicates that a partner is more focused on words used than what they mean. Sure, it would be nice if every time we communicated, we picked exactly the right words, the right tone, and the right timing, but that's something that can only happen when we remove emotion, context, the immediacy of speech, and also our entire shared history with one's partner. As two people build history with each other, they start to make emotional and contextual bridges in their stories. When the stories are pleasant and happy, they elicit feelings of connectedness and comfort. When the stories are conflictual, they may remember all the times they felt a certain negative way and the stories come flooding back. This is why people sometimes "throw everything including the kitchen sink" at each other; some element of their shared story was triggered in what one partner said, which set the other one off. Our communication is a montage of experiences, feelings, understandings, and reactions. We react before we can stop and we analyze all the complex parts of our responses to ensure that our partners are getting the message we're trying to send—and more importantly, that we ourselves agree with the message we're trying to put out there. How many times, after a fight or a misunderstanding, have you said something like, "I know that's what I *said*, but it's not what I *meant*"?

Sometimes we just need to stop for a moment, gather our thoughts, and check ourselves and our reactions before we press forward. Ensuring that *we* agree with what we're saying is the first step toward being a stronger communicator.

In dealing with sexual issues, I often recommend that couples have a "safe word" or phrase, something that both partners agree on and which means, "I need to stop *right now.*" For the same reason, I advise I couples to have a safe word or phrase during communication, too. I like the word "casaba melon." Let's face it: if you're having a challenging conversation and someone yells "casaba melon," you're going to pause pretty quickly (and you might even laugh together for a moment). Often, it just takes a quick moment to regather your thoughts before you can continue in a meaningful way, and the short break allows you to ensure that you are not misspeaking your truth. Taking the time to reset means that it's less likely you'll have a communication meltdown.

When I first start working with a couple, I spend a great deal of time learning how they communicate and what their skillset is. For the first few weeks, we don't even try to delve into their story as a couple; we only work on building up their skills. Before they start a deep dive about all the problems, challenges, and fears they're facing, I want to ensure that each partner can hear and comprehend the other's stories without causing more undue friction for the couple.

Use Your I's

In order to grow, people in committed relationships have to start by talking. When we're frustrated, we are often known to take our partners down in barrages of judgment and correction that are wrapped up in angry tones and high energy. But spouting off about behavior and reactions is never going to change things, because in a supercharged, anxious environment like that, the message can't possibly get in. Instead, when couples talk, they have to learn to speak from the "I" perspective, using phrases like, "I feel," "I want," "I need," "I experience," and so on. When they're doing this effectively, couples might say things like, "I feel frustrated when you leave dirty dishes on the counter," or, "I need you to start rinsing your toothpaste spit out of the sink when you are done in the morning," or, "I love it when you surprise me at lunch!" The key is the I-statement, because you are talking about the frustration, the need, the desire, that *you* feel. The focus becomes your *reaction* and the impact *on* you, rather than you yourself.

The listening part is even more difficult. Listening is not about us at all; it's about the other person. When we listen, we have two very important jobs at the same time: to bear witness, and to expand the story.

Bearing witness means that we are giving honor and credence to what we are being told, and to the person sharing the story, shifting our focus from ourselves to the other person. We do not make the story about us; instead, we focus on *them* and *their* experience, completely. Doing so requires that we keep from becoming defensive, trying to fix the problem, and "helping" (like we discussed in Chapter 1). We keep from predicting what they'll say next because we believe we've heard the story before; we keep from judging their story in any way (good/bad, appropriate/inappropriate, right/wrong, etc.) and from the distraction of strategizing about what we will say the next time they take a breath. When we do any of those things, we become focused on ourselves—*our* reactions, *our* story, what's going on with *us*. Many people find it extremely difficult to take themselves out of the story, especially if they're being referenced as part of it. But just being referenced in the story doesn't give someone permission to own the story. It isn't theirs; the story belongs to their partner. Bearing witness means that we're attending to the story, listening intently, and allowing ourselves to experience the world of the other person, with no reference to ourselves.

The second job in listening is *expanding the story*, and is much more challenging. Expanding the story means inviting your partner to get it all out. If you've ever tried to clean the kind of mold that grows on the backsplash behind the kitchen sink, you know that if you just wipe it away with a paper towel, it grows back. To really deal with it, you have to get in there with the cleanser and search around until you've gotten it all. Tough conversations between partners work the same way. When we find ourselves having the same argument over and over again, it's because we didn't get it all the first time.

Expanding the story means that we must use our curiosity to ask questions. Many people will sit silently and nod their head to show they are listening, but there's a problem with that model of listening: you could be doing your grocery list in your head and the storyteller would never know. Some people repeat back key words and phrases from the other person's story, but simply giving back the same language doesn't show understanding, it shows that we can regurgitate language. We've got to go beyond these listening methods and actually prove to the storyteller that the message has been received, which involves asking for *more* information and context. It's not an interview, an interrogation, or a cross-examination, and it's not about asking yes-no questions or looking for simple answers. But it *is* about going for the deep meaning beneath the story.

There are many different questions we could ask, but here are a few possibilities:

Questions to Show That You're Listening

- ➤ What did you hope or expect would happen?
- ➤ How does that affect you now?
- ➤ If you could change what happened, how would you change it and why?
- ➤ What is the most important thing I should know about this story?
- ➤ What do you wish you had known?
- ➤ What do you wish you had done instead?
- ➤ When did this start to bother you?
- ➤ On a scale of one to ten, how important is this concern to you?

Often when I'm facilitating the Couples by Intention group, I'll wait until one person has shared a thought or experience, and then I'll ask the other members, "So, what are you curious about?" It's a cue that we should all do a personal check-in to see where there might be room to learn something new, check our understandings, or be influenced by what's been said. It's also a reminder that someone shared something personal and that there should be an appropriate acknowledgment of the vulnerability that was just shown, in order to maintain a sense of safety in the group.

Learning to do this can be quite daunting, especially when people in the group might be triggered by what has been shared. To help group members learn this skill, I use an exercise called the Listening Hour.

The Listening Hour

The Listening Hour exercise is a great way to learn basic intimate relationship communication. When both partners want to practice how to tell a story from the "I" perspective and how to listen fully, this exercise allows them to honor their partner.

Each partner invites the other for a Listening Hour date. It needs to be in a time and place where there are no distractions (not in a noisy location or where the kids might distract, and almost certainly away from electronics, for example). First, the partner who sets the date will invite a story from the other. This is done with a broad invitation like, "Tell me a story about . . . " or "Tell me about a time when . . . " The request should be broad. For example:

➤ Tell me a story about when you were a child. What did you think adulthood would be like and how did the reality match that expectation?

➤ Tell me about the first time you realized that you had personal power and could influence others. How did that change you?

➤ What did you think sex was going to be like? How did reality match the expectations?

➤ What do you wish you had been told about being a woman? How might your experience as a woman have been different if you had been told?

As the storyteller shares, the listener "expands" the story by asking questions such as, "What happened next?" or, "What did you hope would happen?" or, "What did you learn from that?" or, "Has that ever happened again?"

If the listener starts to help, fix, or do any of the other internal jobs that prohibit bearing witness, it's appropriate for the listener to ask for a moment to reset or for the storyteller to gently remind the listener that this is "my story." When the story feels complete, the listener asks, "Is there anything else that you think I should know, or are there any questions that you wished I had asked?" It's important that the storyteller feel resolved at the end of the story. Close the exercise with, "Thank you for sharing your story with me."

If the storyteller wishes, they can ask, "What did you get out of my story? What is different for you now?" This question is especially important if it's a story that had been shared previously. I remind couples that the person sharing the story today is not the same person that shared the story previously; what's different this time?

On a logistical note, I recommend that only one story be shared at a time. Set different times for stories so that each individual that is allowing themselves to be vulnerable can relish in the joy of being heard!

For members of Couples by Intention, the Listening Hour becomes a weekly exercise. When they are first starting to practice it, they go for low-hanging fruit, simple stories such as describing something that happened on the way to the meeting. Picking an easy, light narrative allows group members to practice their listening skills without having to be challenged by being part of the story.

It's important to practice these skills several times before moving on to stories about the relationship. As these skills at curiosity mature, group members are better able to use them with each other and in their intimate relationships, especially when dealing with emotionally charged topics. During an argument or in the midst of a period of disconnect is not the time to start trying new skills. That's why we practice in advance, so that when the tough stuff does come up and the stakes get higher, the couples will already have practiced what to do to stay calm and stay together.

The Four Buckets

When we talk about feelings, we typically talk about them in four buckets: anger, sadness/depression, anxiety, or happiness. Most people tend to dump all of their feelings into just one of them.

That's part of why learning to listen means focusing on more than just the spoken word; listening means taking in mood, tone, body language, and every other way that we communicate with each other in order to figure out which "bucket" the other person is using. Too often we make assumptions about the message we are getting, without considering these nonverbal modes of communication, so we have to learn to factor them in. We have to learn to think about *how* things are being said, rather than just *what* is being said.

Without a sense of curiosity, we often stick with whatever interpretation is easiest and assume that it's correct. If your partner is using a loud, stern, definitive manner of communicating, you might assume that anger is the feeling that is being communicated, even if it's not—like in Sam's experience of Yolanda from Chapter 4. If we don't question our assumptions, we might get it really wrong, like Sam did when he failed to consider Yolanda's Italian culture of speaking loudly even when she wasn't angry. This is the classic relationship fight escalation.

▼

Without a sense of curiosity, we often stick with whatever interpretation is easiest and assume that it's correct.

▲

Person A: You are so angry right now!

Person B: I am not!

Person A: Stop yelling!

Person B: I'm not yelling!

Person A: Just calm down!

Person B: Don't tell me to calm down!

An escalation nearly identical to that one played out at Couples by Intention during a conversation on how to manage change. Emilio and Mark have a loud and energetic style of dealing with contention within the relationship, and they each tend to be reactive when stimulated. Here's part of their exchange in our group session, referring to a conversation they'd had earlier in the week:

Emilio:	He was so angry! I didn't even know what I did!
Mark:	Wait—what? I wasn't angry!
Emilio:	Oh, yes, you were! Man, you yelled at me for, like, five minutes!
Mark:	I wasn't yelling. And I wasn't angry!
Emilio:	Oh, please! All I did was ask how your day was, and you exploded all over me.
Mark:	I did not. If you can't handle the answer, don't ask the question!

Have you ever had an interaction like that with your partner? In situations like this one, curiosity needs to extend beyond words into the *means* of communication. When Mark denied being angry with Emilio, Emilio didn't believe him, so I turned to Emilio and said, "Mark says he wasn't angry. Is there anything that you are curious about?" Emilio took a moment to think. "Okay, Mark," he said. "I clearly don't get it. So, what was that all about?" Only then was there an opening for growth and learning.

▼

Anger gets misidentified all the time.

▲

Anger gets misidentified all the time. Lots of different feelings can be perceived as anger: hunger, frustration, tiredness, fear, tension, confusion, loneliness, and feelings of being disrespected can each look like anger, just to name a few. The same is true for perceptions of happiness. For example: think about what happens when someone laughs at a funeral. Stress and discomfort can often come out as giggling, smiling, joking around, and other behaviors that might look like happiness, even though it isn't. Distraction, exhaustion, overdoing things, and physical illness can each be incorrectly interpreted to be anxiety. Likewise, fatigue, exhaustion, and deep thoughtfulness can each be misinterpreted as sadness.

In their situation, Emilio was able to express curiosity with Mark and ask him what was actually going on. The real question that Emilio was asking was this: "You sounded angry to me, so if you weren't angry, what were you feeling?" Mark then shared a story about what had happened to him at work when an important deal fell through—how he felt ineffective and was worried about making his financial goals for the month. He spoke of how he was ultimately afraid of letting Emilio down, because the outcome of the deal would affect both of them financially. Mark had been so challenged with his own story that when Emilio engaged him, his feelings had taken over. If Emilio had known that part of the story earlier, his reactions and engagements would most likely have been different. But Emilio had been responding to what he'd thought was anger, which only made the situation escalate. If he had been able to identify and respond to the fear, belittlement, and other feelings that Mark had felt, the conversation might have looked like this instead:

Emilio: How was your day? Are we still going out tonight?

Mark: It sucked! And no, I am not going out tonight.

Emilio: Wow. You seem angry.

Mark: I'm not angry!

Emilio: Okay, you're not angry. Can you tell me what you are, so I can get it?

Mark: I feel like crap! My deal fell through, and my boss wasn't happy and made sure to let me know about it. It was a horrible day.

Emilio: Sounds like a bad day. Is there anything I can do?

Mark: No.

Emilio: Okay. Why don't you take some time to settle in? I will be in the living room. Can I check on you in 30 minutes? Let me know if there is anything I can do for you.

▼

It is human nature to respond viscerally when faced with strong emotions from a partner

▲

It is human nature to respond viscerally when faced with strong emotions from a partner, because we feel implicated in our partner's reactions. We might feel that we caused the reaction or that we are responsible for managing the reaction (helping). If our partner appears angry, sad, anxious, or happy (the four "buckets"), we probably have an immediate, go-to response. But if whatever response comes to us naturally only seems to decrease our connection to our partner or to increase contention or amplify a challenging situation, we should consider the moment an important one for curiosity, for getting to the bottom of what's actually happening in the situation. Check the assumption! It's a good idea to try something like, "You appear really angry. Am I getting that right? No? Okay—can you tell me what you are feeling?"

Learning a skill like checking in with your partner will take practice, but it comes easier with time. For now, take a moment to reflect on the following questions in your journal.

Journal Questions

What's In Your Bucket?

Pause for a moment and reflect on these questions in your journal. Think about the four buckets of feelings: anger, sadness/depression, anxiety, and happiness. In each category, list three or four other feelings under each category that could be mistaken for the feeling listed. (For example, someone may *look* angry but *actually* just be tired—so write "tiredness" under the "anger" bucket.)

1. Anger
2. Sadness/depression
3. Anxiety
4. Happiness

My Heart Is Late to My Brain

One final lesson on working with feelings and assumptions. I was once treating a high-conflict couple who desperately wanted to learn to handle their fights in a more controlled manner, because they had been fighting in front of Raven, their six-year-old daughter. Through a family session talking about how to handle disagreements in a more controlled manner, Mom and Dad agreed that they wouldn't explode in front of their daughter anymore. But at the end of the session, the daughter wasn't showing relief or acceptance.

Mom was concerned. "It's okay," she said to her daughter. "We figured out how to solve the problem and everything will be better. Cheer up!"

Without missing a beat, Raven said, "I know, Mama, but my heart is late to my brain."

▼

"My heart is late to my brain."

▲

Raven's comment is one of the most insightful things I've ever heard in my office. Perhaps you know what it's like to have a disagreement intense enough that you still feel awful in your body even after you've each come to resolution. In situations like that, one part of your being has finally gotten to a place of Yes but the rest of you remains at No, and it takes time for your systems to regulate back to calm. In those situations, it's important to allow yourself and your beloved to process the experience through mind, heart, body, *and* spirit, all of the various quadrants of your being, before expecting either of you to return to an integrated center of Yes!

Bradley and Carol first entered their couple's therapy not sure how to reconnect in their marriage. They had long held some seriously strong assumptions about each other, a fact that was feeding them into a marriage of quiet disconnect. For too long, they had been feeling isolated, wanting more from their marriage but at a loss as to how to create those opportunities. To get to the bottom of the issue, we worked hard on developing and strengthening curiosity skills. They practiced a Listening Hour every week, taking turns inviting each other to share their story—in reality, inviting them to become active in their marriage once again. Their sense of isolation slowly faded over time as they learned to communicate with more intention, and as they became more curious about each other, they started to sense how hard it really was to bear witness to each other.

Part of what they discovered was that they had become very familiar with the mistake of personalizing everything the other person said. "It was so hard not to feel guilty every time she said she was lonely," confessed Bradley after a particularly tough week. "All I could think of was how I keep letting her down and how I suck as a husband." Conversely, Carol was able to respond, "Telling my story in this way made me realize that I had to make better choices if I wanted more from Brad."

What all of the couples learned through the Couples by Intention group was that communication is about more than just telling people things. If you want to feel real connection with someone, you have to really care that they understand the message you are trying to give them—and that you understand their message. You have to learn that curiosity is a skill and has to be nurtured and developed just like any other. It may feel awkward and transactional to be curious at first, but these are new skills, and if you practice and stick with them, you'll learn over time.

It's also important not to take things literally without first checking to see whether your partner is actually speaking literally. That rule applies not only to the particular words that are used ("I know that's what I *said*, but it's not what I *meant!*") as well as feelings involved ("You seem angry, but if you're not, what are you actually feeling?"). The emotional part of intimate partner communication is the part that trips us up the most. Remember, even if you've found a common understanding and resolution, the heart may be late to the brain, so it's important to leave time and space for the two parts of you to reconnect!

If you are entering into this work because you are feeling disconnected from your partner or because you are struggling with how to communicate with intention and curiosity, or perhaps because your relationship just feels hard right now, it's important to remember one key idea: there's no wave of good feelings that will simply wash over you because you started this work. In reality, what you will probably start to experience is a slow diminishment of the negative experiences and feelings that you are trying to minimize, but it doesn't happen all at once. If you and your partner are consistent in practicing the skills, you will begin to communicate with greater connection and understanding. You'll also be set up well for prioritizing your needs, so that you're both fresh enough to give and receive the attention and care that your relationship needs.

We'll look at that kind of prioritization in Chapter 6. Before we turn there, though, stop for a moment to do the journal exercise like usual.

Journal Questions

Chapter 5 Reflections

Now that you've read Chapter 5, take out your journal again and spend a little time responding to these questions. After reading Chapter 5:

1. What will you *keep doing* in your life and relationship that you are already doing?
2. What will you *start* doing, based on what you learned?
3. What will you *stop* doing?
4. What will you *think more about*?

6

First Me, Then You–Why Self-Care Matters

In this chapter, you will:

- Learn that in order to care for others, you have to put yourself first

- Explore the idea of creating "sacred space" with your partner

- See why it's important to draw boundaries around your relationship

Why Am I Exhausted?

Emilio and Mark often came into the group talking about how great their kids were and what life with rambunctious elementary school kids was like. Emilio described the demands of coaching his son's soccer team, and Mark lamented the constant need to focus on homework, manage playdates, and keep to some semblance of a healthy routine for the kids. Emilio and Mark tended to arrive at the last minute for most sessions, often apologizing for being late, though they weren't, and needing to take a few minutes to settle as they were usually quite rattled from rushing to do so many things just to make it to the group. Emilio and Mark were devoted and loving parents, and they also prioritized their attendance in the group to make sure their marriage was healthy—but they were tired almost to the point of exhaustion.

As you might have guessed from Emilio and Mark's story, one of the greatest challenges that Couples by Intention partners talk about each week is how to take care of everybody and everything—what we call this *the "Me Versus We" dilemma*. It's the constant search for healthy boundaries and clear communication so that both partners can understand the limitations of connection.

It's often one of the most difficult lessons to learn as we want to be "merged" with someone we care about. We want to be unified, but chasing that desire can ultimately lead to a sense of weariness, a loss of resiliency, and a shortness of temper. In a group session focused on parenting, Meili once talked about the plan that she and John had put in place to start trying to have children, and her concerns about what it would actually mean for her. "I know that having kids is really what I want," Meili said. "I've never doubted that. But I'm wary, because I already feel stretched out and I don't know if this thing that I want so much will also be the thing that breaks me. I know that John will be a great dad and an equal parent, but I have so much already and I don't want to miss anything."

Carol was quick to jump in with her own experience. "I hear you," she said. "That's exactly where I was. The truth is that even with Bradley being a great dad, I still feel that I have to do everything and be responsible for everything. I'm exhausted all the time! By the time I finish dealing with all the crap at work on an average day and finally get home, I immediately get thrown into kid-pickup and having to manage whatever emotional drama their undeveloped selves can't manage yet. And even if dinner *had* already been thrown into the crockpot, I'm facing another three hours of laundry, bath time, paying the bills—you name it. If Bradley isn't jumping in and doing his part, I have to be the bad cop. We have agreements on how all of this is supposed to happen, and when it doesn't, I get angry, and then I start to feel guilty for chastising him and sounding like a total pain in the ass. If he is doing something fun or relaxing, I get resentful because I start to wonder, 'When is it ever my time?' I start keeping score like I expect it to be tit for tat, even though I don't really believe that.

"Don't get me wrong," Carol continued. "I know it's worth it. I don't want to sound that I am complaining or that I don't love my life. It is just that I feel so completely wrung out sometimes with the 'joyful' life I've built!"

"That sounds so confusing to me," said Meili. "I'm concerned that John and I already have a hard time finding 'us' time. How do you do it?"

"That isn't the biggest problem," replied Carol. "The bigger problem is finding 'me' time! What I have come to understand is that parenting, household management, paying the bills, and all the other pressures are not 'us' time. Then I have to figure out how to make hard choices. Do I spend time paying the bills, tending to the kids, or paying attention to my husband? I often have to figure out who is saddest or neediest or most critical, and then hope there is no fallout from the choice I make about whom to tend to. None of this makes me feel connected to Bradley. There is a difference between the We with a capital 'W' and the we with a small 'w.' I have really come to understand in the last few months, though, that there is no way for us to figure out the *We* if I haven't figured out the *me*."

"Oh, I know that's true," exclaimed Meili, as everyone else around the circle nodded their agreement.

What Meili and Carol were really talking about was prioritizing their lives. So many of us get overrun by our responsibilities to the things we want and the people we love that we work ourselves straight into the ground. When we're worn down, we aren't able to give what we want and what our relationship requires in order to grow and strengthen. After managing all of our responsibilities and trying to attend to the needs of our relation-

▼

So many of us get overrun by our responsibilities to the things we want and the people we love that we work ourselves straight into the ground.

▲

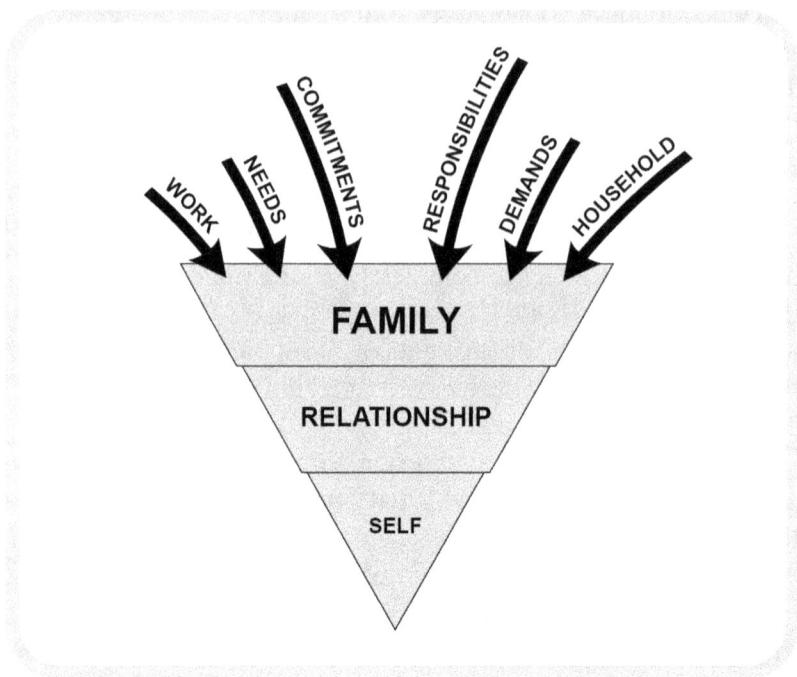

Figure 6: The Upside-Down Triangle

ships, it is highly unlikely that there is anything left inside us for taking care of ourselves, and when we can't take care of ourselves, we can't be present for all the responsibilities we take on. We end up driving ourselves into the ground.

It's a no-win situation, and I describe it to the group as the "Upside-Down Triangle" (see Figure 6).

The top tier of the triangle, *Family*, contains all the responsibilities that we are constantly trying to juggle: raising children, managing our extended circle of relatives, running the household, keeping a high level of performance at work, and other day-to-day things. They combine to fill the space of this tier until there isn't any "oxygen" left in a person's life. We tend to describe the quest to handle all these things with terms like "work-life balance," but very few of us seem to be able to figure out how to get things to equilibrium.

▼

Very few of us seem to be able to figure out how to get things to equilibrium.

▲

If there is any energy that remains after the outside and family needs are met, it tends to be put into the *Relationship* tier, which is where we respond to our partners and try to be available to them. This includes communication, emotional availability, problem-solving, planning for the future, making decisions, and sex and intimacy. Finally, if there's anything left over, which is unlikely, we think about ourselves—the final tier, which we call *Self.*

Does that sound exhausting? I felt tired just describing those things in writing just now! There's a good reason: the upside-down triangle shows a top-heavy structure resting on a very fine point. If a structure were to look like this in real life, it would be very easy to topple it over into a disaster!

When I draw this image on the board, I ask group members what they put in their top tier. Their answers often include kids, carpool, aging parents, paying the bills, needy bosses, work travel schedules, and other outward-facing requirements. When I ask about the Relationship tier, people talk about a partner's desire for sex when they themselves are exhausted, or needing to talk, wanting to plan, or asking for support. When describing the Relationship tier, members of the group talk about these factors in a way that sounds like they are being drained more, instead of experiencing the relationship as a source of connection and rejuvenation.

The bottom tier, Self, is usually a struggle for the group. Most members talk about having very little going on in that space. Carol reported that taking bubble baths to escape was the one thing she did for herself. She often made her baths so long, in fact, that she'd be sitting in cold water by the time they were over, simply because bathing was the only time when Bradley and the kids would leave her alone. Sam reported that he was often volunteering to do more than his share of chores because he could do them alone, and while he felt pressure to do even more than he does, chore-time at least allowed him to be by himself without feeling guilty.

The upside-down triangle model doesn't work for members of my groups. One time, I asked them what it would be like if they were to flip the triangle over—if the new way of thinking were to be "me first," like in Figure 7.

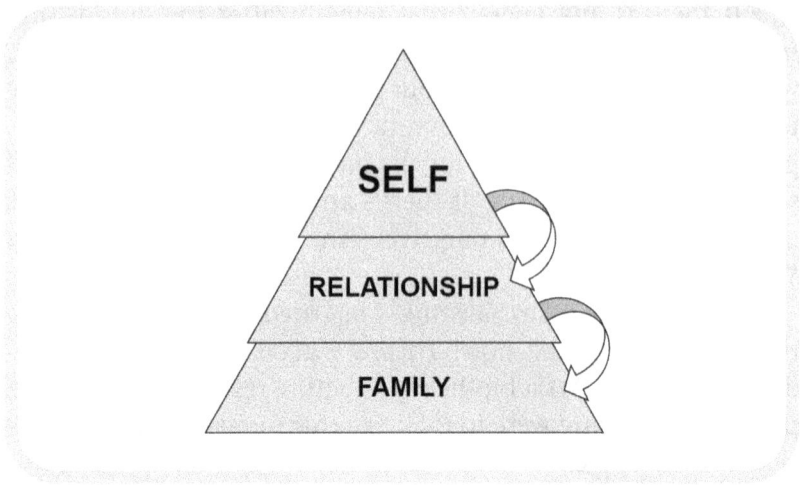

Figure 7: The Right-Side-Up Triangle

What if each person were to say, "I take care of Self as my top priority, because if I can't take care of me, then I can't be there for you"? Think of how much better the relationships could be if each person were to say, "It's my responsibility to ensure that I can show up fully for this relationship. That doesn't mean that I'm so self-centered that I don't care about anyone else or that I shirk my responsibilities. Rather, it means that I must ensure that I am healthy and operating at the top of my game. I must be comfortable saying 'no' at times. I must eat right. I must get good sleep. I must take care of my body and manage my stress, anxiety, and any other personal concerns that affect me. In other words, I must be centered—mind, heart, body, and spirit—so that I can be fully present for you."

If you're in a relationship, think back to when it first started. The person you idealized at that time was someone who could show up for you. You didn't feel that you got a drained-out, washed-up partner. Neither did they; why would your partner want that in you? Somewhere along the line, you might have begun to live a life that was increasingly more complicated, whether through increased responsibility at work, additional children, a change in your health, or some other event. Whatever happened, your life might have become more complicated, but your coping and self-care stayed exactly the same. You didn't change your tactics as your situation changed. You were trying to do more with less.

Taking Care of Yourself

That's why self-care is an essential skill in learning to relate well to another person. Self-care may look like going to therapy or the gym, taking time to take a class or read a book, or doing yoga or meditation—whatever is refreshing to your body and spirit. It means ensuring that you are managing your physical and mental health. When I asked the group what they would want in the Self tier on the triangle, they had no problems naming all the things they would put in there. Sam talked about working in his woodshop in the basement, Yolanda talked about Pilates, Mark mentioned learning the guitar that he bought but never played, and John spoke of going back to school.

If we took the time to take care of ourselves, we would be more likely to stay present for our Relationship (the second tier). And if each partner is showing up for the Relationship, then everything else that falls into the bottom tier of Family will be more manageable. After trying out the new approach for a few weeks, the group members reported that turning the triangle upside-down also allowed them to be better role models for their children, have a more unified front as a couple to their families, feel more financially secure, and take better risks. Best of all, several of the couples found time and energy for sex and intimacy!

"I never thought about it in this context before," said Yolanda during one session of Couples by Intention, "but when we first started dating, we had a 'Don't Fucking Tell Me What to Do' rule. We both wanted independence and to make our own decisions. We were clear that we couldn't manage each other's lives or control the other person, so the rule was our way of saying, 'I need to take care of myself and I expect you to make your own decisions. This relationship has to work for me before it works for us.'" Sam concurred. "Yeah, I mean she has a shit-ton of art supplies that I could care less about," he said, "but making art makes her happy. We did have to talk about her getting a better space to put it all, but that is her thing. When I wanted to get a drone, I got a drone. I am a grownup and I can do that for myself."

Now Us—The Importance of Sacred Space and Boundaries

But even flipping the triangle over doesn't solve the whole dilemma of having enough energy to be together. "Okay," someone might say, "so we prioritize self and then focus on our relationship. Fine. But how do we make the relationship work when *no one else is paying attention to our priority*? It sure would be great if the whole world were just to fall in line with our plans for how we are going

▼

"I wish I could just build a wall around me and my partner for a weekend."

▲

to manage all of this juggling, but that's not how real life works. What are we supposed to do?" Emilio summed it up one night at Couples by Intention when he said, "I wish I could just build a wall around me and my partner for a weekend." Everyone's heads nodded in agreement.

What Emilio was really talking about is something every relationship needs—a wall, of sorts, or what I call the need for sacred space.

Sacred space can be a physical place, a ritual, or a special, meaningful activity that gets scheduled. It is the place and time where only the two of you get to be. Children, work, electronics, the PTA, mothers and in-laws, and cell phones are not allowed into the sacred space. Wherever you pick, and whatever you do, it needs to be the time and location where the two of you intentionally focus *only* on each other and on the health of the relationship. I share with the group that in my home, the sacred space is our bedroom. Our children are never allowed into it, and over the years, it has become a thing of mystery for them. They know, from having been reminded so many times, that they have full run of the rest of the house but that our bedroom is the only place that is off-limits. For us, it is the place where we can openly have emotional and physical intimacy, where we can argue in private, and where we go when we need to heal and sometimes just to be alone.

Sacred space does not have to be a place for sex, although if it helps to facilitate great sex, then so much the better. The most important thing is that it's a place or ritual where both partners can put an intentional focus on the relationship, stepping back from worldly distractions and responsibilities. It's the place where your children are not allowed, which helps your children learn that your relationship with your partner is separate from your relationship with them. For that reason, it also serves as a model for the children as to how to prioritize an intimate relationship above all others.

One couple I worked with, Ellen and Brandon, relished the idea of creating a space in their house that would be for them, and they returned the following week talking about how their adolescent children were upset that they were being kicked out of their parents' bedroom. They couldn't understand why they couldn't just go in there to watch television, talk on the phone, or to go rummaging for clothes. The couple started laughing when they explained their children's reactions. Ellen said, "It felt so good to take our space back. It was like pushing away an invading army!"

▼

"It felt so good to take our space back. It was like pushing away an invading army!"

▲

Other couples spoke of *ritual* as their sacred space. They described starting a regular date night, or rituals around walking the dog, or having a regular massage night, and other ideas. Carol and Bradley relished being in bed on Sunday mornings, listening to NPR and doing the crossword puzzle. They gave their kids a digital alarm clock and told them they needed to play in their room until the clock said "10." Only then could they come to get Mommy and Daddy.

Sacred space can be quite difficult to implement because it requires resetting expectations with children, friends, family, and even oneself. It's important to remember that creating sacred space is like yoga, meditation, or listening; it's a practice that must be intentionally observed all the time, and which takes practice to implement.

Sacred space also creates a boundary that keeps your children safe. When children are too intimately involved in their parents' relationships, they develop a sense of being a third partner. Children often feel responsible for the experience of the parents, resulting in their becoming "parentified," trying to take care of one or both parents as they see challenges and try to resolve them on their parents' behalves or in their stead. Younger children do not have the cognitive development to process such adult concerns, and older children should be launching into their own adulthood and will struggle to do so if they feel they are needed at home to manage their parents' lives, even if they are no longer living at home. Relationship intimacy between partners is challenging at best when this level of parent-child enmeshment exists. Creating sacred space helps to solve this, allowing for healthy boundaries that allow children to feel more secure and opening pathways to more intimacy between the adults.

Now it's your turn to think about what sacred space could look like in your life and with your partner.

Journal Questions

Sacred Space

For this journal exercise, spend a few minutes thinking through these questions and writing some answers in your journal:

- Think about *yourself as an individual*. What would sacred space look like for *you*? What are some places, spaces, or practices that make you feel nourished and healthy, or that provide a restful reprieve from the demands of everyday life? (A room in your house? A park in your neighborhood? A pastime, like exploring country roads in your car, playing a sport, or spending time with friends? A meditative practice, like yoga, worship, or massage?) Name a few, and remember that there are no right or wrong answers, so long as they're authentic to who *you* are.

- Now think about your *relationship*. How could you and your partner create sacred space for each of you and your relationship? What would best serve your needs? Remember, there is no right or wrong way to create sacred space as long as it works for both partners!

- If you were thinking of creating a *physical* space, is it in your home? Does it have to be your bedroom? What will you use the space for? Could it be a particular venue that you both appreciate, like the beach?

- What might your sacred space look like if it were a *ritual* instead of a physical space? How would you make it sustainable? (Don't set yourselves up for failure! If going out every Friday night is just too unmanageable due to the needs of your family or job, don't set that expectation. Maybe start smaller—like Sunday morning coffee, for example—and grow your sacred space from there!)

Conversation Exercise: Sacred space would be a great topic for a Listening Hour (see page 133). Try saying something like this to your partner: "Tell me about how you envision sacred space in our relationship. What would it look like and what would you want to get from it? What would it mean to you to be able to have a space where only you and I could go?"

Boundaries—An Example

When the group was talking about parenthood one night, John described the challenge he felt growing up. "My parents struggled all the time," he said. "It was clear to us what every fight, conversation, and make-up session was about. My sisters and I felt like we were in the middle of their marriage. My mother would align with my sisters and try to get them to agree with her. My father would isolate himself, and I felt obliged to reach out to him because my sisters were being so tight with my mother. There was never any mystery to our parents, because all five of us were in the marriage."

Meili chimed in. "When I first met John's family," she said, "I was so confused. I didn't have a mother growing up, so I didn't really get the whole 'everyone-in' dynamic. I kept saying to John, 'Why do your sisters keep getting all in your parents' business, and why do they keep trying to get you to manage your dad? It isn't your job!'

"We had many conflicts about this the first year and a half we were together," she continued. "It wasn't until John started talking about not understanding intimate boundaries that we were able to do some work in therapy on how to create them—and not just with his parents, but how we wanted our *kids* to have a different experience."

Another way of thinking of boundaries came from Ethan and Valerie, who told the group about a repetitive argument they kept cycling through. They explained it from both perspectives, which inspired others to speak up as well.

Valerie: Ethan and I struggle with being really intentional in how to achieve goals. I'm not sure why, but we talk about the goals, we agree to the goals—and then it all falls apart. There is either a lack of execution, which pisses the other off and we get into these crazy arguments, or there is a totally lame attempt that only feels like shitty lip-service. It's like he tells me "yes!" but his actions tell me "no!" Then I find I have to keep going back and back and back because I start getting kooky, crazy with frustration. Then I start thinking, 'Did I make this up?' and 'Who am I to have this much management and say over us?' It makes me feel out-of-control. We keep talking about being intentional and we aren't doing that. But I am curious to know why! We need to solve this!

Ethan: She's right. That's exactly what happens. It makes me crazy, too. We start to talk about something, and it all sounds right, but it can often start to fall apart so quickly. If I don't respond or act or perform the way she wants me to, then I am wrong, I have failed. I start to feel that she over-runs me and I have no space. I don't need her advice or her critique.

Emilio: We used to do the same thing. It drove me nuts. I was just like you, Valerie. Mark would agree to a goal, and then I would be sitting there waiting—and nothing. Or it was only halfway there, which is not what we agreed to, and I would just feel the heat come over me. I felt like if I didn't do it or push him really hard, we would never get anywhere. I would start to resent him for not working hard enough. It took me a long time to start to acknowledge that maybe he was working to his 100%, and that his 100% was not the same as my 100%. When I started to realize that, I could give him more space.

Mark: He's right. That was a hard time for us. The part for me that was shocking was when I began to realize that I did agree to the goals that we made. I thought they were good goals and I wanted them. I just didn't hold them to the same intensity that Emilio did. I thought they were good goals. He thought they were critical goals. We didn't see them the same way.

Ethan: Mark! That's it! That is exactly what I have been trying to figure out how to say! Valerie, I do agree with *our* goals. I just don't agree with the same intensity that you do. When you come at me with that level of intensity, I start to shut down. It is hard for me to be intentionally working on goals with you when I feel this enormous pres-sure of importance being pushed on me!

Valerie: Yes. And I'm realizing Emilio also has some-thing. My 100% doesn't match yours, Ethan, but I want it to. We have to learn to talk about our goals differently—not just what they are, but how strongly we feel about them and what we are willing and able to do to make them happen, and we aren't going to be equal. Intellectually, I get it, but I also know that it's going to be hard to do emotionally. I get caught in goals as silos. I look at a task, and I just want it *done*. It seems so easy, but I also know there are things competing against it, and I lose track of that when I just want to get something done. I get so laser-focused on it.

Ethan: We can do this. I have to be more intentional about talking about how strongly I am supporting and agreeing to goals, and I also have to be better at letting you know when I think you are crossing my boundaries with intensity.

This was a magic moment in the Couples by Intention group for several reasons. It really showed how one couple's experience can enlighten another's. More importantly, it talked about how the second tier of the triangle, Relationship, is about securing boundaries around and between the partners. The power of intentionality was the foundation that allowed Mark and Emilio to be mindful about what was happening to them and what allowed Valerie and Ethan to be curious enough to want to solve their ongoing conflict. I often remind couples in the group that if you are having the same conflict dynamic over and over again, you haven't resolved it. This is the time to increase curiosity about the dynamic so that there is more room to be intentional, resulting in the emergence of a new dynamic entirely.

Put Everything Else Where It Belongs: At the Bottom

The third tier on the Right-Side-Up Triangle is *everything else*. The parents in the group initially struggled with this, articulating a sense of guilt for not being more present and attentive with their children. Several of them were concerned that if they put themselves first, they would screw up their children or make them feel unloved. But the couples without children challenged those with children (and the conversation became *electric* with ideas and wisdom being shared from person to person and couple to couple). As parents talked about the pressure to do more, attend PTA meetings, go to games and lessons, monitor homework, and any number of other commitments, their increased agitation and stress were clearly visible.

The non-parents in the group were quick to notice it and comment. Emilio described a time when he had spent his entire weekend changing his plans because his son's game time was moved, resulting in a loss of Emilio's free time to complete more on his honey-do list. Yolanda jumped in. "So, why did that happen?" she asked Emilio. "Why did you try to fit more in? If you were planning on time for yourself in the afternoon, why didn't you just take that time in the morning? Was there a reason that the schedule couldn't just be flipped?"

Emilio was taken aback. "I never thought of taking personal time in the morning," he said, "because I am always on morning-kid-duty, so I just looked at the huge list of things I had to do and started doing them."

I remind group members that the third tier contains anything that is *beyond* their relationship, and while children do belong in the third tier, it's possible to segment the tier even more. For example, a couple might choose children and pets over extended family, or house chores over social engagements. Each couple must learn to be curious and intentional about what they include in their third tier. They must negotiate and very carefully decide what the tier looks like, or it will just become like that awful junk drawer that everyone has in their kitchen, full of stuff that we think we need but never get to. When we do look at it, we get turned off and just shut the drawer again.

After this conversation, Ethan and Valerie began to change the way they set goals. While there was always still a barrage of little things that needed to get done every day, they began to save their big-ticket items, such as major chores, weekend plans, financial decisions, and so on, for a weekly planning meeting. At their weekly planning meeting, they would talk about what needed to be done and why, as well as how it would be done and by whom. That conversation began to include a conversation about how *important* each item was to each of them, so that appropriate expectations could be set between the two partners.

Through talking through the Triangle in the Couples by Intention program, and practicing it over time, Ethan expressed feeling a greater sense of peace and control. "Learning to talk about why things need to be done and how strong we both feel about them was probably one of the biggest take-aways from this whole process," he said.

Self-Care Matters

Couples who are trying to be stronger, closer, and healthier require structure, which is one thing that weekly conversation can help to provide. Being fully present and capable in your relationship requires that you maintain a regimen of self-care. No one wants to be in a relationship with someone who is constantly stressed out, worn, and depleted. When you can be fully present in your relationship, you have a greater ability to show curiosity and intention! Imagine how you might be able to take on the world if you felt that your relationship was strong, supportive, and a source of energy, rather than just another drain on you!

Creating sacred space and holding boundaries is a tremendous part of building a strong relationship. Every relationship needs a space to grow and thrive, something special that is protected from the pressures of the world, and which can be a haven for rest in the good times, and a place for healing in the hard times. The act of creating and maintaining boundaries is critical if you want meaningful sacred space. The healthiest relationships have the clearest boundaries, and the boundaries are where you set them.

▼

The healthiest relationships have the clearest boundaries, and the boundaries are where you set them.

▲

Wrapping Up

In this chapter, we've taken stock of the fact that we all feel exhausted from time to time—and that most of us tend to think in terms of the "Upside-Down Triangle," which puts family first, then the relationship, then self. But the best way to make *everybody* healthiest is to start with self, then move to the relationship, and *then* family and the rest of life. We also talked about how to create "sacred space," whether it's physical or some kind of regular ritual, and the importance of creating boundaries around that space.

As the members of Couples by Intention get further and further into the twelve-week season together, they practice boundary-setting, like we've discussed in this chapter—which helps them to feel even safer with their partners than they did before. Then they learn to incorporate the idea of being safe with one another into an even further step: unpacking some of the assumptions that each partner brings into the relationship. This helps them to think carefully about how to attain the benefits each couple desires from getting close to one another. We'll dive a little deeper into these ideas in Chapter 7. First, though, it's time to take stock of what you'll do with what you've learned in this chapter.

Journal Questions

Chapter 6 Reflections

Having read Chapter 6, open up your journal again and write out some responses to these questions. After reading Chapter 6:

1. What will you *keep doing* in your life and relationship that you are already doing?
2. What will you *start doing*, based on what you learned?
3. What will you *stop doing*?
4. What will you *think more about*?

Identifying Connections: See It! Do It! Learn It! Get the Rewards!

In this chapter, you will:

- Explore why assumptions can harm a relationship—and how to figure out what assumptions you're bringing into your relationship

- Think carefully about what it is you want to achieve in the relationship in the first place

- Design a way to come home from work each day that shows intentionality to your partner

Bradley and Carol's story is fairly typical. When they first came to my office, they were a couple who cared deeply for each other but felt completely disconnected. There was not a lot of outward anger between them, nor were they fighting all the time. They had the kind of quiet, simmering disconnect and lack of communication that left each of them unsure of what the other thought, and so they did what most couples do; they filled in the gaps with assumptions about what the other person was thinking.

Carol would talk about how Bradley didn't want sex and intimacy, because he never initiated, which Carol took to mean that Bradley didn't find her attractive anymore. When presented with this assumption, Bradley was almost dumbstruck. "Carol, you are the most beautiful woman I know," he said. "I still look at you and think, 'Damn! She looks good in those yoga pants!' I don't know why I don't just do something about it—but it isn't about you. Trust me, you're still hot as hell!"

In another session, Bradley shared that he believed Carol was ashamed to be married to someone in alcoholism recovery, that it was more than she originally thought she was signing on for. Carol was stunned at the assumption. "Don't you get it?" she protested in session. "I am so *proud* of you! You've been so courageous and brave to face your addiction head-on. I know it is ugly, but I never signed on for pretty, I signed on for *real*. Why do you think I am still here? If it were more than I could handle or wanted to handle, I wouldn't be here."

Bradley and Carol's story is an example of why uncovering assumptions together can be a strategic relationship skill, another way to expand your curiosity about each other. Unless we learn to recognize when we're assuming things about our partners, we're likely to live out of ideas that simply aren't true, creating conflict or tension that might not otherwise be there. But like any other relationship skill, it takes sustained practice to learn how to unpack and dismiss assumptions before they get large enough to do damage.

Deadly Assumptions and Meaning Motivations

Assumptions kill curiosity. When we start to live a relationship with the assumption that we *already know* such-and-such about our partners, we will naturally start to feel less curious about each other. For that reason, it's safe to say that assumptions are dead ends. When we assume, we stop asking for new information about the other person, and we start avoiding anything that we think has the potential to be uncomfortable in our discovery of the other. The more we live in the past, and the more we hold on to false assumptions about what the future can be, the more limited our curiosity about the other person becomes and the more "closed" we become to discovering them. My friend Julia Balaisis, a fellow therapist based in Toronto, once told me that "assumptions are the direct opposite side of curiosity." In other words, you can't be curious if you're busy making assumptions about your partner.

▼

You can't be curious if you're busy making assumptions about your partner.

▲

People in relationships often make assumptions based on the behaviors we witness in them and the literal words our partners use. Many times during my couple's therapy, one of the partners has said (to the other) something like, "You don't care" or "You never listen to me," which are actually classic assumptions: how do you *know* that the other person doesn't care? Can you prove that the other person is never actually listening? Once those assumptions are spoken, it usually takes about a nano-second for the other partner to try to negate those sentiments, or to shut down because they are so frustrated from *trying* to listen and still not being recognized for their efforts.

In moments like these, I remind my clients that no one can "see" things like listening, trying, or caring. Energies spent on those activities are internal, happening *inside* the other person, and your partner doesn't have X-ray vision no matter how badly you wish they did. Your partner can't see what is going on inside your head, your heart, or your body, and they can't see what motivates you to act a certain way. People can only see and react to the *behaviors* you are actually exhibiting outwardly, not the reasons behind them, and sometimes our behaviors can give very confusing messages— the crux of the age-old challenge of making our behaviors match our intentions.

To make things even more complicated, the partners in a relationship might have similar intentions but vastly different behaviors, which is what I often call the "Salt and Pepper" dilemma. Here's the example I use.

The Salt and Pepper Dilemma

Let's say that a bunch of friends go out to dinner at a family restaurant, and everyone shares a similar desire for their dining experience: to have the option to season the meal with salt and pepper. But when the friends start to look around for the condiments, they find that there are no salt or pepper shakers on the table. From this moment forward, the guests start acting differently from one another, each in pursuit of the same simple goal: putting salt and pepper on their food;

> ➤ Some folks decide that the absence of the salt and pepper shakers isn't a problem at all; they simply get up, go to the next table, grab the salt and pepper, and come back and continue eating without issue: problem solved, no harm done.

> ➤ Other guests also resign to the absence of the salt and pepper, but for them, there *is* an issue, and they resolve that their tips will reflect the poor service!

> ➤ Still others will start to feel bad for the servers, whom they see are working hard while staying quite pleasant in spite of the demands on them, and they resolve not to bother the servers with additional requests (and they'll tell themselves that salt probably isn't good for the diet anyway).

> ➤ Still others start to look around at the other diners, trying to see if *they* have salt and pepper, to determine whether there might be some special process for being given salt and pepper.

The Salt and Pepper Dilemma is one example of how two or more people can share the exact same desire while using vastly different behaviors in order to get there. In the observance of these differences of behavior, many assumptions are made about what the individuals think, believe, and need, and about the different ways they experience desire for the same thing. In the scenario, each diner had the same goal: ensure that their goal of having salt and pepper was met at the moment that they wanted it. Any individual diner could have looked at any other person's chosen method of dealing with the missing salt and pepper and *assumed* that they were working toward a different goal. The people who went to another table could have looked at the inaction of those who decided to accept the missing condiments and concluded that they were lazy or didn't share the goal of wanting salt and pepper, and the others could have assumed that the proactive folks were being uptight and spoiled. Each of those assumptions would have been wrong; the goal was simply to cope, and the various guests chose different ways of doing it.

Challenge Assumptions!

In relationships, it's important to challenge assumptions early on. One of the early homework exercises I give the couples is to try to name the assumptions they make about their partners. The more we can bring assumptions into the open, the more we can challenge them for understanding and clarity and throw out the ones that aren't true. I remind couples that assumptions can be positive, negative, accurate, or inaccurate—and in all cases, we should challenge them.

Sam and Yolanda had come to couple's therapy for premarital counseling before they were part of Couples by Intention. On one particular occasion, they came in quite agitated with a simple story that expressed the power of assumption. It was a cold New England morning and their appointment was very early, and for this story, it's important to note that Sam and Yolanda aren't morning people!

The night before our couple's session about wedding planning, Sam and Yolanda had a difficult discussion in which Yolanda asked Sam to talk to his best man about some logistics for the Jack and Jill wedding shower that was being planned for them. Yolanda, who had been neck-deep in wedding planning, was looking forward to the shower, but Sam, who wasn't keen on the idea of a shower at all, told Yolanda that he would ask. A few hours later, Yolanda overheard Sam talking on the phone to his best man, telling him that he didn't want the shower to begin with, and that he was feeling quite negative about it.

Yolanda was crushed. She had dreamed about her wedding shower from the time she was a girl. How could Sam not know how important this moment was? The next morning was that cold, New England-style winter day here in Massachusetts. On the drive to the session with me, Yolanda turned the car's heat up to "high" because she was cold, and Sam immediately reached over and turned it off without a word. For the rest of the short ride to my office, the air in the car was thick with silent rage and anger between the two of them. It was clear to them that something was wrong, and when they walked into my office, *I* could tell without asking that some kind of discord was happening between them at that very moment.

It didn't take long for it to come out. "He doesn't care about me," began Yolanda. "He totally disrespected me. I turned on the heat and he immediately just reached over and shut it off!"

"It was blowing ice-cold air on my feet," countered Sam, stunned by her outburst. "I wanted the car to warm up first. I wasn't disrespecting you! I was *cold*!"

Because of their unfinished business from the day before, Yolanda and Sam had been unable to articulate what had been going on during their episode in the car, and they started making assumptions about the other person's motivations and their sense of value to the other person. The lack of communication had created an even greater chasm between them than had opened up during the misunderstanding over the wedding shower. After we had processed through the reality of what the conflict was really all about, Yolanda admitted that she assumed that Sam would be excited about the shower and would show the same level of anticipation that she did. Sam didn't realize what the shower meant to Yolanda, and he was dreading it personally and let his anticipation of discomfort overcome him. Ultimately, they were able to negotiate a shower experience that met both of their needs, with Yolanda at the center of attention and Sam lovingly supportive in the background.

Uncover What You Assume

When I work with couples caught in assumption, I lead them in a shared exercise to name and challenge their assumptions. I draw two columns on my whiteboard: "Assumptions I have about my partner" and "Assumptions my partner has about me." I then ask the couples

Table 1: Assumptions	
Assumptions I have about my partner *(examples)*	**Assumptions my partner has about me** *(examples)*
➤ He is committed to our relationship ➤ She would never cheat on me ➤ He chooses his mother over me ➤ She is not interested in sex anymore ➤ He only sees me as a housemaid, cook, and laundress ➤ He thinks I am angry all the time for no reason ➤ He thinks I'm fat	➤ I am no longer attracted to him ➤ I think he is lazy ➤ I can't handle my emotions ➤ I tell my friends personal things about him ➤ I am controlling ➤ I love him ➤ I am a good parent ➤ I struggle to manage my emotions

to list out the assumptions that might fall under each list, bearing in mind that they can be positive or negative, accurate or inaccurate.

I often facilitate the exercise by asking my clients, "What do you know is true about your partner, and what's true about what your partner thinks about you?" Assumptions often feel like facts until we reflect on them, and so as my clients start to answer the question, I follow up with, "Is that a fact or an assumption?" If it turns out to be an assumption, we put it on the list and move on to the next one. If the client says it's a fact, I will ask their partner to confirm that it really is one. If both agree, we move on and don't engage in it. (I also remind them that this isn't the time to go into a back-and-forth about whether something is a fact or not. A simple yes-or-no response is enough to get something on the board. I remind couples that there will be time later to be intentional and use curiosity to find out why something is a fact or an assumption.) Table 1 is an example of this exercise in action.

After we've made the lists, I ask questions like these:

> ➤ Are there any assumptions that you have about your partner that give you pause?
> ➤ What are you curious about?
> ➤ What assumptions that you think your partner has about you do you feel are inaccurate?
> ➤ Would you like to challenge any of the assumptions you listed?
> ➤ How were the assumptions created?
> ➤ Are the assumptions your partner has about you based in your behavior?
> ➤ Why do you think your partner has those assumptions?
> ➤ How might you know if your partner really has those assumptions?

Once we can name our assumptions and begin to challenge them, we can intentionally start using curiosity as a strategic relationship tool. I encourage couples to continue to ask things like, "How is my curiosity present today?" and, "Do I share my curiosity with my partner?" and, "Do I see curiosity from my partner?" and, "How would I notice it?" Every one of the assumptions listed could be the basis of a Listening Hour (see Chapter 5) on its own!

The purpose of the exercise is to get couples out of their heads and into an intentional conversation with their partner. Many Couples by Intention participants have reported that their ability to challenge assumptions has been one of the foundational skills they've learned, allowing them to be more present and active in their relationships. They also said that uncovering assumptions requires a huge amount of courage, because some of the assumptions can feel very private or personal, triggering the insecurities of one or both partners and uncovering the need for deep personal growth.

"Learning to name my assumptions was one of the hardest parts of being intentional," said Bradley one night, "because it meant that I would have to face the fact that a lot of the growth needed to come from me if I wanted more from Carol. It was easy to just assume that Carol was one way or another because it absolved me of my responsibility. In many ways, it was comfortable to just sit there and wait for her to change and acknowledge my understanding—but it never happened. Couples by Intention taught me that I need to be intentionally challenging myself, my assumptions, and my ability to be brave, if I want a better relationship."

▼

"Couples by Intention taught me that I need to be intentionally challenging myself, my assumptions, and my ability to be brave, if I want a better relationship."

▲

Journal Questions

Assumptions

What work can *you* do using this book to name, challenge, and perhaps alter your assumptions in your own relationship? Take a moment to complete the journal exercise below before we continue further.

1. What assumptions do you have about your partner?
2. What assumptions do you think your partner has about you?
3. *Why* do you think your partner might have those assumptions?
4. In what ways could you check to see if your assumptions are accurate?

Understanding Connection

The Couples by Intention program teaches couples to understand what makes for a meaningful relationship. The answer is unique for every couple, which means that there is no single relationship model that fits everyone. Using curiosity with one's partner to find what is meaningful is the only way to lead to a deeper connection, because each relationship's pathways to better connection and deeper intimacy will be as unique as the partners themselves. Even though there isn't one model that fits every couple, curiosity is a way for any couple to find *their* unique model.

Along the way, a couple's lack of insight and skill can lead to confusing behaviors and difficult conversations. That's why a well-developed sense of curiosity is crucial for defining what the goals for the partnership look like and what skills the couple needs to develop in order to attain what they want together.

Many people do not have insight into what "ownership" of a relationship entails. The majority of couples in my practice say things like, "The relationship just developed over time and before you know it, there we were." A statement like that shows no sense of ownership—the feeling you are making the relationship happen—or being intentional about charting the course that the relationship has taken. Couples who operate without a roadmap, shared goals, or a deliberate, nurtured sense of curiosity about each other—in other words, most of us—find ourselves on a wild, often enjoyable ride with our partner at first, until the ride stops and the inherent fun or sense of novelty fades away, as it always does. It's the couples who do the work of *developing* curiosity about each other, even when it's no longer thrilling to do so, that survive the doldrums that come with any relationship and even come to enjoy each other more over time. Learning how to merge curiosity and intention isn't just a good idea; it's the key to opening up a new world of possibility for being a couple. It's where to look for success and connection.

Why Do We Even Want Connection In the First Place?

It's become apparent to me over the years that most couples have a clear and distinct vision of what a connected relationship would look like, how they would experience it, and how it would appear publicly—but they don't know how to make it actually come about. Early in the relationship, many couples become frustrated because they've unconsciously been comparing themselves to the romantic ideals they've seen in movies, books, TV, and social media, and they've sensed that their relationship doesn't look like any of those. As soon as those pop-culture ideals start to feel unattainable to one or both partners, which they usually do, a sense of dissatisfaction sets in because the relationship isn't growing into that romantic ideal.

Table 2: Connection	
See/Experience	

To deal with that growing sense of frustration, I offer a brain-storming experience for couples to do together in my office. I begin the exercise by writing the word "Connection" at the top of the board, and I draw lines below it to divide the rest of the board into four equal spaces. In the first box, I write the words "See/Experience" (see Table 2).

Then I ask the couple: "If you and your partner were strongly connected, what would you notice or see in terms of the observable?" I also ask them to be sure that the things that they name are behaviors and identifiable reactions more than abstract concepts and feelings. It's perfectly acceptable if partners list items that they don't share or agree on, because the exercise isn't about finding agreement, but about discovering what each partner experiences.

"Think broadly," I tell them. "What you may notice is that it may actually be the *absence* of a behavior that would let you know that connection was happening—like not looking at your devices. Stop to pause and reflect. What do you notice?"

The goal here is simply to name what comes to mind—to brainstorm as honestly and freely as possible. Since it's important for both partners to share their thoughts and experiences at each stage of the exercise, I facilitate it the first time, meaning that both partners work together to answer the questions without editing, judging, or critiquing any responses that the other partner gives. The goal is to understand the totality of experience for each partner.

Common items listed in the "See/Experience" box include:

- ➤ Not interrupted by electronics
- ➤ Eye contact
- ➤ Laughter
- ➤ Feeling comfortable in my body
- ➤ Wanting the time to continue
- ➤ Showing desire
- ➤ Not trying to leave
- ➤ No distractions

- ➤ Not being at a loss for words
- ➤ Physical contact
- ➤ Time flies by quickly
- ➤ Flirtations
- ➤ Decrease in stress and anxiety
- ➤ I am focused on the here and now
- ➤ I am confident
- ➤ I am heard

The list can get quite long as couples start to identify their personal imagery of a connected relationship. As couples start to feel that they have named all their identifiers for connection, I let them know that they can come back at any time and add more to it, and we move to the second box, which I label, "Do" (see Table 3).

In the "Do" box, I ask couples to name what actions they think that they must take as individuals so that they can experience the type of connection and experience they detailed in the first box. It's a question of responsibility and ownership; it's not about what they want from their partner, but what their individual work might need to look like. The point also isn't whether they think they *can* do these things—whether they think they're skilled enough or ready—but purely what would need to be done for the level of connection they want, if skill and experience were no object. Some of the items might be quite literal and observable (like "put your phone away") while some might be more contextual (like "have good stress management"). Don't be surprised if you find yourself feeling overwhelmed by the amount of work it takes to create a strong and meaningful connection! Know that it's okay to identify things that need to be done, even if you don't know how to do them.

Couples then begin to name things such as:

Table 3: Connection

See/Experience:	Do:
➤ Not interrupted by electronics ➤ Eye contact ➤ Laughter ➤ Feeling comfortable in my body ➤ Wanting the time to continue ➤ Show of desire ➤ Not trying to leave ➤ No distractions ➤ Not being at a loss for words ➤ Physical contact ➤ Time flies by quickly ➤ Flirtations ➤ Decrease in stress and anxiety ➤ I am focused on the here and now ➤ I am confident ➤ I feel heard	

- ➤ Make time
- ➤ Not focus on old arguments
- ➤ Disconnect from electronics
- ➤ Forgive
- ➤ Listen
- ➤ Be present
- ➤ Take care of my body
- ➤ Prioritize this moment
- ➤ Be curious!

- ➤ Be more intentional
- ➤ Compartmentalize
- ➤ Do not assume or act on assumption
- ➤ Plan ahead
- ➤ Not eat a large meal at lunch so I don't feel bloated and gassy
- ➤ Have a suspension of disbelief that connection can happen

What couples begin to notice in the "Do" box is that it's a lot of work to have a great connection. The box can feel overwhelming as the list of work it takes to be in a connected relationship grows. After filling in this second box, couples often want to go back to the first one and add more material there, which is a great practice.

I then move to the third box and label it "Know/Learn" (see Table 4).

In this third box, I ask each partner what skills, knowledge, and abilities they need to develop so that they can do the activities they listed in the second box in a regular fashion, in order to experience their desired connection as defined in the first box. Look at all the items in boxes 1 and 2, and consider this question for box 3: "What do you need to know/learn/grow so that those items can happen in reality?" I urge couples to focus on themselves and their own skillsets, and *not* to use it as an opportunity to critique their partner.

Each partner usually starts out by talking about their personal growth goals and the areas where they feel they need support and guidance in the relationship. To interact honestly with box 3 requires humility, a strong sense of self, introspection, and the ability to take risks. Think of box 3 as a golden box of opportunity. The items listed here can be folded into a learning plan to support each partner as they seek greater ownership of the relationship. Typical responses for box 3 include:

Table 4: Connection

See/Experience:

- ➤ Not interrupted by electronics
- ➤ Eye contact
- ➤ Laughter
- ➤ Feeling comfortable in my body
- ➤ Wanting the time to continue
- ➤ Show of desire
- ➤ Not trying to leave
- ➤ No distractions
- ➤ Not being at a loss for words
- ➤ Physical contact
- ➤ Time flies by quickly
- ➤ Flirtations
- ➤ Decrease in stress and anxiety
- ➤ I am focused on the here and now
- ➤ I am confident
- ➤ I feel heard

Do:

- ➤ Make time
- ➤ Not focus on old arguments
- ➤ Disconnect from electronics
- ➤ Forgive
- ➤ Listen
- ➤ Be present
- ➤ Take care of my body
- ➤ Prioritize this moment
- ➤ Be curious!
- ➤ Be more intentional
- ➤ Compartmentalize
- ➤ Do not assume or act on assumption
- ➤ Plan ahead
- ➤ Not eat a large meal at lunch so I don't feel bloated and gassy
- ➤ Have a suspension of disbelief that connection can happen

Know/Learn:

- ➤ Time management
- ➤ Priority management
- ➤ Forgiveness
- ➤ Communication
- ➤ Risk management
- ➤ Assumption management
- ➤ How to talk about my feelings
- ➤ How to unplug
- ➤ How to have one conversation at a time
- ➤ Anxiety management
- ➤ The ability to let go of the past
- ➤ The ability to differentiate this relationship from past relationships
- ➤ Learn to be intentional

Notice that much of what is listed in box 3 in these examples looks very similar to what is listed in box 2. That typically happens in practice, too. In other words, the very work we must do to create meaningful connection turn out to be the things that we haven't been taught yet and don't feel confident doing. Each item becomes an opportunity to set a new course—to decide, "*This* is something I want to invest time and energy in learning how to do."

In the fourth box, I write the word "Rewards" and ask each partner something like this: "Imagine that you've learned and mastered everything you listed in box 3, that you could start consistently doing everything you wrote in box 2, and that you were experiencing the deep level of connection you defined in box 1. What would the rewards for that effort be?" (See Table 5).

This question often takes people by surprise. They talk about understanding the importance of connection, and they describe desiring it with their partner, but thinking of connection in a deeper context and its impact on the overall experience is a new question. In other words, Box 1 is not the ultimate goal or prize: that's Box 4!

This question creates a stronger commitment to the work of building intentionality and curiosity into the relationship. Rewards begin to look like the overall quality of life, an image of what deep intimacy and connectedness means to the individual partner.

Table 5: Connection

See/Experience:	Do:
➤ Not interrupted by electronics	➤ Make time
➤ Eye contact	➤ Not focus on old arguments
➤ Laughter	➤ Disconnect from electronics
➤ Feeling comfortable in my body	➤ Forgive
➤ Wanting the time to continue	➤ Listen
➤ Show of desire	➤ Be present
➤ Not trying to leave	➤ Take care of my body
➤ No distractions	➤ Prioritize this moment
➤ Not being at a loss for words	➤ Be curious!
➤ Physical contact	➤ Be more intentional
➤ Time flies by quickly	➤ Compartmentalize
➤ Flirtations	➤ Do not assume or act on assumption
➤ Decrease in stress and anxiety	➤ Plan ahead
➤ I am focused on the here and now	➤ Not eat a large meal at lunch so I don't feel bloated and gassy
➤ I am confident	➤ Have a suspension of disbelief that connection can happen
➤ I feel heard	

Know/Learn:	Rewards:
➤ Time management	
➤ Priority management	
➤ Forgiveness	
➤ Communication	
➤ Risk management	
➤ Assumption management	

Table 5: Connection (continued)	
Know/Learn:	**Rewards:**
➤ How to talk about my feelings ➤ How to unplug ➤ How to have one conversation at a time ➤ Anxiety management ➤ How to compartmentalize ➤ The ability to let go of the past ➤ The ability to differentiate this relationship from past relationships ➤ Learn how to be intentional	

Typical answers might look like these:

➤ Better sex!

➤ Better intimacy!

➤ Less stress

➤ Ability to take greater risk

➤ Greater self-confidence

➤ Feeling like I have greater value

➤ More financial stability

➤ More trust

➤ Better sleep

➤ More support

➤ Better role modeling for the kids

➤ Better able to focus at work

➤ Better self-image

➤ Longer life

Take a look at the example listed below in Table 6. These are just some of the answers that couples put in their boxes. In the Journal Exercise for this chapter, you'll say what *you'd* include.

Table 6: Connection

See/Experience:	Do:
➤ Not interrupted by electronics	➤ Make time
➤ Eye contact	➤ Not focus on old arguments
➤ Laughter	➤ Disconnect from electronics
➤ Feeling comfortable in my body	➤ Forgive
➤ Wanting the time to continue	➤ Listen
➤ Show of desire	➤ Be present
➤ Not trying to leave	➤ Take care of my body
➤ No distractions	➤ Prioritize this moment
➤ Not being at a loss for words	➤ Be curious!
➤ Physical contact	➤ Be more intentional
➤ Time flies by quickly	➤ Compartmentalize
➤ Flirtations	➤ Do not assume or act on assumption
➤ Decrease in stress and anxiety	➤ Plan ahead
➤ I am focused on the here and now	➤ Not eat a large meal at lunch so I don't feel bloated and gassy
➤ I am confident	➤ Have a suspension of disbelief that connection can happen
➤ I feel heard	

Know/Learn:	Rewards:
➤ Time management	➤ Better sex!
➤ Priority management	➤ Better intimacy!
➤ Forgiveness	➤ Less stress
➤ Communication	➤ Ability to take greater risk
➤ Risk management	➤ Greater self confidence
➤ Assumption management	➤ Feeling like I have greater value

Table 6: Connection (continued)	
Know/Learn:	**Rewards:**
➤ How to talk about my feelings ➤ How to unplug ➤ How to have one conversation at a time ➤ Anxiety management ➤ How to compartmentalize ➤ The ability to let go of the past ➤ The ability to differentiate this relationship from past relationships ➤ Learn how to be intentional	➤ More financial stability ➤ More trust ➤ Better sleep ➤ More support ➤ Better role modeling for the kids ➤ Better able to focus at work ➤ Better self-image ➤ Longer life

John and Meili did this exercise with me during one of their sessions. After they were finished, John couldn't believe what they had just accomplished. "I can't believe that we did this exercise in only 40 minutes!" he beamed. "I think of our marriage so differently now!"

I asked him what was different. "So many things," he said, "but the big thing is that it helped me to remember that the answers and solutions are in me. If I could just learn to slow down and ask better questions, I would get better solutions!"

Meili was pleased, too. "For the first time, I think I really get what you mean about being curious," she said. "I have to be curious about me as much as I have to be curious about John. I don't know why, but I never put that together before this."

The Connection exercise often has that kind of deep impact on couples as they learn that their connection isn't just about their partner not showing up or not giving them what they need: it's about their *own* stake and investment as well. Couples often say things like, "I have been working so hard at this relationship, but I realize I haven't been working in the right way," or, "All this time, I have been looking at why my partner isn't making me feel connected and I just got a reality check: I'm not making myself available for connection!"

From Connection to Intimacy: How to Come Home

Finally, once the couple has completed the Connection exercise, I ask them to change the word at the top from *Connection* to *Intimacy,* and to do the exercise a second time. "How does that change the conversation?" I ask them. "How do you define the difference between *connection* and *intimacy*? What would the boxes look like if the word *Trust* were at the top? And what other words would you put at the top to start a meaningful conversation with your partner?"

Once couples have learned to use this tool to discover what they are looking for and what it requires, I give them a homework assignment focused on connection. I ask them what happens at the end of the workday when they return home, which yields answers like, "I drop my bags and start cooking dinner," or, "I yell, 'Hey, I'm home!'" or, "We start our night, whatever we have to do." What is apparent to me is that couples are not normally in the habit of reconnecting the relationship when they walk in the door at the end of the day. Each partner tends to move forward with an understanding that everything is the way it was when they left that morning. But I remind couples that they may have lived a whole *life's* worth of changes in the time it took to go through just that one workday. They have faced challenges during the day, met new people, solved problems, and been faced with new realities. It's important to catch up and plug into each other to see what's changed in the other person's life, because it's often the case that the person whom you encounter at 6:00 in the evening isn't the same person that you said goodbye to at 7:30 that very morning.

Typically, one partner comes home before the other (or has already been home during the day) and begins to get involved in some activity, whether it's cooking dinner, watching television, or working some more, which means that when the second partner enters the house, they enter to activity already in progress. But I ask the couple to enter the house differently. When the second person enters the house, the first partner home should take a quick break from what they are doing, and each partner should intentionally greet each other in the following way.

First, there should a mutual, physical display of affection, whether it's a hug, a kiss, or some other kind of touch. Remember Chapter 4, when we talked about babies and their failure to thrive if they're not touched? As adults, we're the same: we crave touch in varying degrees. Touch can be healing and magical, and having nonsexual but intimate touch can be remarkably grounding, especially when two people are being reintroduced to each other after an entire day's worth of change.

The touch should be accompanied with direct eye contact and a mutual, verbal welcoming that sounds something like, "I'm so glad you're home" or, "I'm happy to be home" or, "I missed you today."

Next, there should be a quick check-in from both partners. This isn't meant to be an in-depth conversation, not at this stage—just a simple question to take the temperature of how each partner feels, so that the other partner can start to anticipate any care that might be needed during the evening. It's important to know any essential information that might change the direction of the night. For example: "How are you tonight?" "Is there anything you need tonight?" "Is there anything critical that I need to know for tonight?" "Are you at 'thumbs-up' or 'thumbs-down' tonight?" Once this check-in happens, both partners can get back to whatever activity they were engaged in, or set about doing what helps them to get settled into their evening routine. This entire check-in process might take a total of 15 or 20 seconds. That means that if you are cooking dinner, helping the kids with homework, or working at your laptop, the diversion isn't long enough to completely derail you, and the amount of connectedness and foundation you'll get from the check-in should make the break from your activity worth it!

If couples could get into the habit of simply welcoming each other back to the relationship after periods apart, they would have a greater sense of connection and a better read on what might be needed throughout the course of their time together between coming home and going to sleep.

What about you? What's your coming-home routine? How might you alter it to express connection and intimacy with your partner? Take a moment to complete the journal exercise below before we go further.

Journal Questions

Welcome Home!

In your journal, write some answers to the following questions:

1. How long does it take for you and your partner to feel connected after coming home at the end of the day?

2. How are you greeted when you come home?

3. When your partner comes home, what is it essential for you to know?

4. What is hard about changing the way you greet each other after work?

5. Write out some ideas of what you think coming home to each other *could* look like. What would you like to see/hear/experience that would help you feel chosen?

Making a New Rhythm

It almost became expected that Emilio and Mark would come crashing into the group room at the last minute, as was their reputation amid their hectic lives. But something started to shift around week eight of Couples by Intention: they started to show up in the waiting room a few minutes early, and they appeared relaxed and ready for the group to begin.

People started to notice. One day at the start of the session, Valerie spoke up and asked, "What is going on with you guys? There's no more big entry!" Mark laughed and said, "That's right. We've really made a commitment to connection. *We* have to be Number 1, and we are starting to prioritize ourselves that way. It's funny, but when we actually connect and are working on the same page, everything seems easier."

I congratulated them and asked them specifically, "So, what's different now?" Emilio said, "We are doing our work. We had to wake up and realize that we were both living in the house and relating but we weren't having a relationship. We had a serious conversation about what we need to do, and part of that was that we needed new skills and new rules. We needed to start acting differently. So we made an agreement to do that work. We don't expect each other to be perfect or for the work to be easy, but we do expect each other to keep working."

Mark and Emilio's new awareness was a critical step in growing their relationship. They shared their conversation with the group, and it became obvious to everybody that the work they had to do was more with *themselves* than with each other. There was a palpable wave of energy within the group from that moment on, as each member began focusing on how they themselves had to check out how honest they were being with themselves. They had to get to a point of being at peace about who they were and what they wanted, and about how they brought these things to their relationship. It was a powerful process, and it came from taking careful stock of what assumptions they were making and what they needed to change about how they thought about themselves and the relationship.

Wrapping Up

In this chapter, we've talked about the deadly power of assumptions in a relationship, and we've practiced uncovering our own assumptions in order to evaluate and either keep or discard them, based on what's actually true. We also did the Connection exercise and described what we actually want out of our relationship, and we practiced re-imagining how we can "come home to each other" in a way that says, "I am here for you." In the next chapter, we'll explore how to balance our individual work with our work as a couple. But first, as always, let's pause and reflect.

Journal Questions

Chapter 7 Reflections

Now that you've finished Chapter 7, it's time to think back on what you've gained from what you've read, and how your practices can change. After reading Chapter 7:

1. What will you *keep doing* in your life and relationship that you are already doing?

2. What will you *start* doing, based on what you learned?

3. What will you *stop* doing?

4. What will you *think more about*?

8

Who Are You, Anyway?– Alignment

In this chapter, you will:

- Explore why it's so important to have a sense of who you are (internal alignment) and to live authentically (external alignment)

- Learn how to watch for "timelines" that others might impose on your relationship without your consent

- Discover why integrity, which is built on alignment, is crucial for your relationship to withstand others' timelines

When Shira and Theresa (whom we met in Chapter 2) came to couple's therapy, their primary concern was how to respect each other's boundaries. "She is just so overbearing sometimes," said Shira. "I feel like no matter what I say or what I want, I get overwhelmed by her energy, and I just don't have the self-confidence to stand up to her all the time."

Theresa was unimpressed. "I can't be someone I'm not, just because she doesn't have self-confidence," she said. "I'm just being me. I don't want to overwhelm her, but she knew who she was getting into a relationship with. Why can't she just tell me what she wants?"

Exchanges like Shira and Theresa's are familiar in my office, as partners try to find the balance between being true to themselves and being accessible to the ones they love, without having to try to be someone else simply to be heard or respected.

Being Who You Are

Many couples come to me when they are struggling with being their authentic selves. They struggle with standing up to their beloved partners with their own truths because they are afraid that their partner won't be able to handle the reality, or that their partner will become angry or leave. They are concerned that if they speak their truth with words and actions, they will have to deal with the fear and apprehension of living a true and authentic life.

▼

In many ways, each of us have to come out, to decide to be the real person we are.

▲

In many ways, each of us have to come out, to decide to be the real person we are. "You can only have a relationship with the person who is in front of you today," I often tell my Couples by Intention groups. "You are no longer in a relationship with the person you met years ago, and you are not in a relationship with the person you hope your partner will evolve into. You must be present, here and now, because this is the only person you can have a relationship with. Your *own* 'here and now' person is the only person your partner can have a relationship with." This means that we must each deeply understand ourselves and the assets that we bring to the relationship when we are most authentic.

The groups tend to work hard to challenge the barriers to being authentic. It's difficult work, because each group member brings their own unique difficulties and fears to the conversation. We spend a lot of time looking at the messages and pressures that make us who we have become. Once the group has had some experience opening up to the differing messages and models that form their assumptions, the next step is to work toward creating what I call *alignment*.

Alignment is making sure that everything fits together in a way that promotes the ability to be successful. It's important to align the

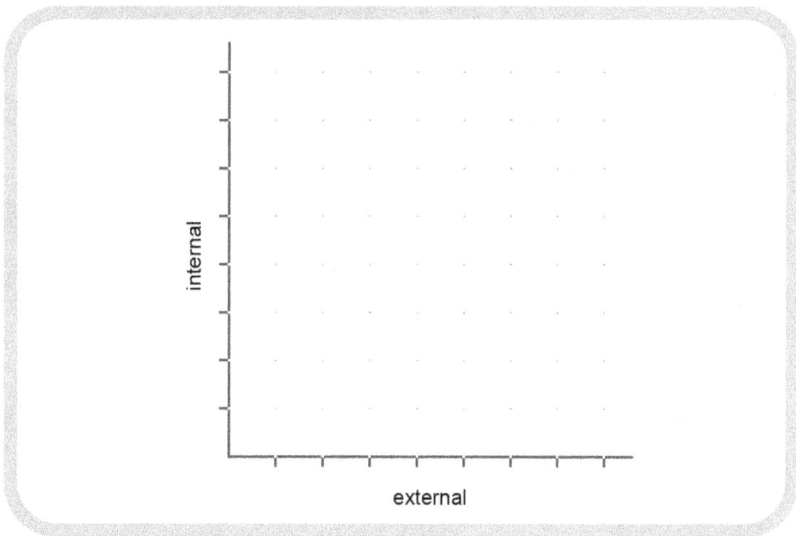

Figure 8: Alignment

tires on your car so that the car can operate efficiently and effectively. Similarly, what would happen if an elevator weren't aligned with the floor when the door opened? Imagine the challenges that could result if the roof of your home weren't aligned to its walls!

There are two types of alignment, and both are equally important: *internal* alignment and *external* alignment. When we look at our own internal and external alignment (which are unique to each person), we begin to get a glimpse into how we engage with the outside world. If we put internal alignment on a vertical axis and external alignment on a horizontal axis, we can begin to look at how our internal and external selves connect (see Figure 8).

To better understand how the intersection works, let's look at each aspect of alignment independently.

Internal Alignment: Knowing Yourself

Internal alignment is about how well we know ourselves—our ability to be introspective and to challenge ourselves to be honest with our life circumstances. For many people, it can be challenging to do this kind of internal observation. Acknowledging our truth

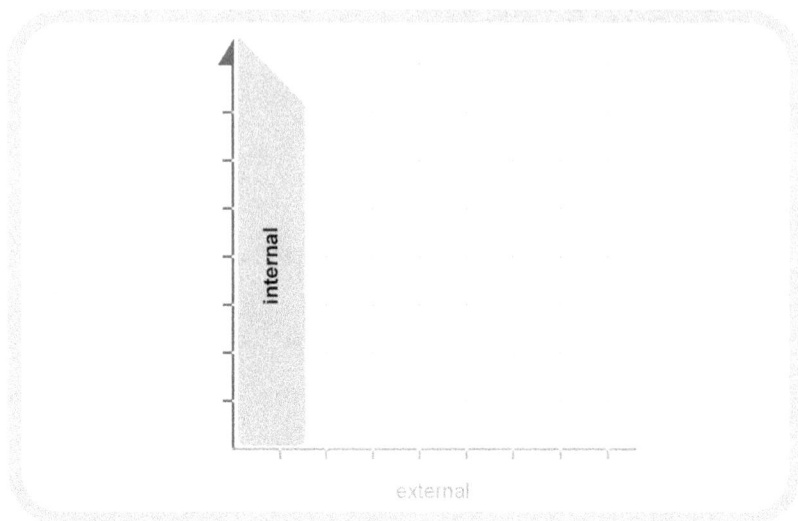

Figure 9: Alignment

requires us to challenge the conventions and messages that we have been given over the course of our life.

Ethan is a great example of how the pursuit of internal align-ment required him to question how he saw himself and every message that he ever received as he grew up. Identifying as trans and coming out to himself meant that he had to build a new aware-ness and truth for himself. All the messages he got as a result of being born a biological female seemed foreign to him. He had to figure out why he didn't align with the messages, expectations, and opportunities that were being presented to him. In other words, he felt "out of alignment," and he spent years trying to understand himself and to find his true sense of self.

As a person gains internal awareness and clarity, they gain greater internal alignment over time. Internal alignment doesn't necessarily mean that we *like* what we learn about ourselves—only that we accept what we know.

In Ethan's case, his journey to self-awareness required him to look deeper into the experiences of his life and how he came to understand them. It meant that Ethan had to be curious about himself and the world he lived in. On a graph, we can show that the more insight and introspective knowledge Ethan gained, the higher up the vertical axis he grew (see Figure 9).

External Alignment: Acting Authentically

External alignment has to do with how we relate to the outside world. Our ability to hold steady without crumbling under the weight of social, familial, relational, and professional pressure determines how strong our external alignment is. Often, as people are faced with negative forces, they find themselves weakened and less able to hold a steady sense of who they are. The conflict of disagreement or lack of acceptance can be too much to bear, and the person can acquiesce to what they think is expected of them. External alignment is about having the ability to rally against those forces—to differentiate from the pressure to conform to expectations. In Ethan's story, his external alignment started to grow when he stopped accepting heteronormative rules and pressures as the only acceptable way of being. His decision to create his own path, regardless of what everyone else thought, was an exhibition of his increased external alignment.

As with internal alignment, external alignment is a gradient scale. The more Ethan was able to hold to his own path, the greater his external alignment and the further along the horizontal axis he found himself (see Figure 10).

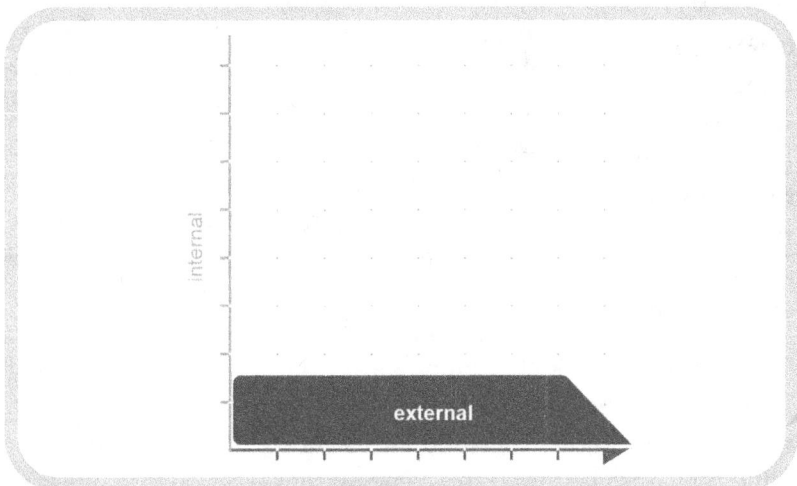

Figure 10: Alignment

Putting the Alignments Together

Once we understand the concepts of internal and external alignment, we can get to the major concerns that are raised in the group. One of the most common questions raised in each group is, "How do I know when I am being truly authentic and not just reacting to old messages?" As Ethan continued to introduce his story to the group, he said that he felt like he was standing on the right stage with the right cast—and "reading the wrong script." It was a wonderfully insightful comment, because it spoke to Ethan's battle between internal and external alignment: what he knew to be true about himself, versus what the world expected of him.

At the intersection between internal and external alignment is what we call "integrity," or the ability to be upright, solid, and values-driven in how we approach the world. We also refer to this as being "whole" or "solid." Think of a house: where is its integrity? It's not in the paint colors or the wallpaper; it's not in the expensive antique dresser that's been in your family for generations. It's not in the flowerboxes or even in the pretty décor or the visible design.

A house's integrity is in the sturdiness of its beams and the quality of its construction. Integrity is the invisible force that allows a house to stand up in a storm against 50-mile-per-hour winds. It's in the weatherproofing, in the insulation that can keep residents warm when it's snowing outside, in the roof that doesn't leak. Just like with the houses we live in, our personal integrity is what allows us to stand up to the storm of relationships and societal expectations. It's what allows us to be real and to speak our truth. It's the point where the intersection of internal and external alignment takes place.

> ▼
> **Our personal integrity is what allows us to stand up to the storm of relationships and societal expectations.**
> ▲

Ethan had to dig deep and build strong self-awareness as he identified for himself that he was trans, and as his internal alignment grew, he had to find a way to come out to the world as his authentic self. The more he could hold onto his truth and come out to the world, the integrity dot on his alignment diagram moved up and to the right—meaning

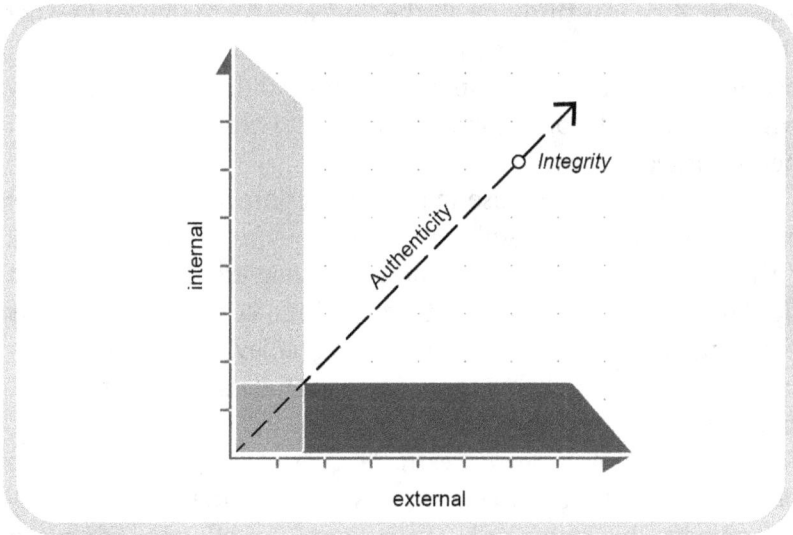

Figure 11: Alignment

that he was also growing in authenticity, showing the world more of his true self and buckling less under the pressure, real or perceived, to be anything but who he knew himself to be. For most of us, the dot constantly moves around the graph as we enter new situations, get challenged in new ways, and find our footings. Every day and every situation has an influence on how far up and to the right our dot goes (see Figure 11).

John reported having a similar experience with alignment, one that began to impact his relationship with Meili. "The more I became aware of the negative messages my parents gave me about manhood and my lack of achievement," he said in session once, "the more I realized that I could make choices about that. The more I made choices, the more I was able to push back against their criticisms. The stronger I felt, the closer to Meili I became. It's not like my parents were trying to be in the middle of my marriage, but they were there just the same. I had to stand strong so that I could build a marriage that I could hold up based on myself, not on everyone else's image of what I should be."

"He's right," said Meili. "I could see a definite change in John when he started dealing with his parents. It was like he would also start talking to me differently—not in a bad way, but I didn't have to guess what he was thinking all the time and try to figure out what the hell was going on with him. It was like he grew into himself and became my husband who spoke his mind, didn't let me get away with things, and stopped letting me dictate him—which is a job I never wanted anyway!"

Bradley and Carol also made connections to the concerns of alignment. "Bradley doesn't talk to me about *his* needs," said Carol. "It's not that I don't want to know, but they are just not brought up. Then what happens is that everything becomes based on my chaos, my life, my work." She looked at Bradley. "It is really important to me that you know that I want to understand your needs," said Carol. "How do I get that?"

Bradley took a deep breath. "I guess I keep going back to default," he said. "The week gets busy, and by the end of the day I don't have the energy or know the words to tell you. I was never taught how to talk about my needs. I know I have them and what I would like life to be, but I was always taught to just work and do and provide. I guess I don't speak my needs because I don't feel like I have the language to tell you, and I don't want to feel that my vocabulary isn't good enough. You are always so articulate and I'm just not."

Bradley's ability to self-assess and to know himself was a strong suggestion of internal alignment, and his growing ability to talk about things and bring them forward to Carol was an example of his growing external alignment. Their ability to connect over those needs showed their growing curiosity and intention; they were beginning to use all the tools in their toolbox!

The Power of Timelines

Another way that alignment shows up in the group is when we begin to talk about timeline expectations, which is a topic that comes up one way or another every time I start a new group. *Timelines are the subtle and not-so-subtle expectations that are given to us from others*, the names and narratives that we take on or rally against throughout the course of our lives. They are the messages that tell us whether we are good or bad, right or wrong, or appropriate or inappropriate as we craft our adult selves.

Carol had had some experience with how challenging time-lines could be. "There were so many expectations that I put on Bradley when we met," she said during one of our group sessions. "I expected him to behave in certain ways to achieve milestones. It took me a long time to realize that the expectations I put on him weren't ones that I wanted. It was all the South."

"I was born in the South," she continued. "The path was given to me by my culture, and it was exceptionally clear. Because I lost my mother at a young age, the importance of the timeline seemed even heavier. I was to graduate high school, then college—and then meet a man and get married. I had to buy a house before I had a child. Then I should have another child.

"There were specific timelines for each phase. My aunts and my friends' parents would openly ask me about how I was working to achieve these timeline goals. They all seemed to be in agreement of the timeline I was expected to follow. I felt like there were no other options."

That last comment elicited a strong reaction from Emilio. "Yeah," he said. "It was no different here. Being born in Puerto Rico, the repeating patterns were clear. The steps to the future were made in stone, and how I was supposed to walk those steps—how I was supposed to behave on the steps—left me with no other options."

At that point, the group became quite lively as each member of the group spoke up in turn about the expectations they faced from others. They were feeling the pressures of external alignment, but they were seeing that the process of discovering *other* ways to the future—pathways that aligned with their *own* goals, identity, and desires—was the start of developing *internal* alignment. Ethan told the group that coming to accept that he was trans wasn't easy, but that the most challenging aspect of his transition was actually in facing the timelines that had been put on him when everyone had understood him to be female. Ethan had had to hold onto his internal alignment while others adjusted their personal align-ments to the new reality that Ethan was male, not female.

Ethan and Valerie had started dating in what Valerie thought was a lesbian relationship, and Ethan's coming out forced Valerie to look at her own alignments to determine if she could continue the

196 Elliott Kronenfeld, Ph.D., LICSW, CSTS

relationship in an intentional and authentic manner. "Deciding to stay with Ethan was not the most challenging aspect for me," she said. "I love him, and our relationship was solid—and he makes me feel safe and loved. Actually, he was able to show me a side of manhood that I never experienced in my life.

"The harder part of Ethan's coming out," she continued, "was that I started to lose my identity socially. Because Ethan passes so convincingly as a male, everyone reads us as a heteronormative couple. But I am not straight! I feel like I started to disappear and I needed change the way I interacted with the world so that I could be true to myself [internal alignment] and manage how I was in the world so that world could see the true me, a queer female [external alignment]."

Relationships grow in strength and resiliency as alignment and integrity develop, and one of the most important benefits of this work is the development of healthy boundaries within the couple. I constantly remind the Couples by Intention group that the healthiest relationships have the clearest boundaries. It's no small task to hold boundaries with a loved one, and nearly impossible when you are struggling with being authentic and holding on to your integrity.

How Boundaries Help Establish Integrity and Resist Timelines

Boundaries, the limits and structures that we put around ourselves and our relationships to maintain healthy interactions, exist on several levels. The No-Helping Rule (from Chapter 1) is an example of a boundary. Establishing sacred space that allows a couple the privacy they need to nourish themselves (from Chapter 6) is also a boundary. Other boundaries might include things like the rule of "leaving work at work," or the expectation to put electronics away at set times, or the definitions that are created through the monogamy scales.

Each of these types of boundaries, and others we can think of, require both partners to maintain a strong personal alignment.

Each partner needs to understand their internal alignment so that they can be intentional about their commitments and be present to one another. They also need to have the skill to manage external alignment so that they can negotiate healthy boundaries that work within the relationship. As couples create these mutually established rules based on how they understand their needs, they create an integrity that is based on *that couple's* alignment.

Here's why it matters, and why we're coming back to the idea of "boundaries" in this chapter. In order to flourish, a couple has to have enough *integrity* (alignment) in order to resist the *timelines* that others will try to impose on them. And in order for the couple to do that—to build integrity into the relationship itself—both *individuals within the couple* have to establish their own integrity first. How the couple understands who they are as a unit and how they will interact with the outside world is determined by the level of *integrity* and *authenticity* within the relationship, which is determined by the level of integrity within each individual. These are what I mean by boundaries.

Plus, as the partners grow in their authenticity, a special type of boundary grows—a sacred one, a boundary that is simply never crossed, such as infidelity. It's understood that the cost of breaking that boundary *may* be repairable, but that the damage would be deep and would leave scar tissue on the emotions of both partners. Each couple defines their own sacred boundaries; they are negotiated, discussed, and well-understood by both partners.

Ethan's journey into his manhood challenged his internal and external alignment, challenged the timelines that society had put on him when they thought he was female, and forced him to reset boundaries with all of his most important relationships.

"I could never be in a relationship with anyone before I came out," he said. "I was struggling so much inside and I was so unhappy with *everything* that there was no way that I could let anyone get close to me. I was so angry and closed off. I wasn't a happy person. I needed to be able to transition so that I could stand myself. Once I came out, I didn't have to live up to anyone's standards but my own. It was like I was becoming my own man."

"Um, dude," said Emilio, "you were!" (Everyone laughed with that!)

Every healthy relationship starts with *individuals*. These individuals must have a strong sense of who they are and what they need if the relationship is to flourish. Couples by Intention is designed to increase each person's curiosity into self-discovery through internal alignment, while also teaching them how to navigate the waters of external alignment in an intimate relationship. As group members begin to show up with integrity (the ability to withstand challenging forces) in their relationship, shared structures such as boundaries, rules, and sacred space can be designed. But all relationships start with the

▼

No relationship is stronger than the lowest common level of integrity between the two partners.

▲

individual, and no relationship is stronger than the lowest common level of integrity between the two partners. At this point in Couples by Intention—as we approach the end of our three months together—we've usually started to see that each individual is going to keep pushing themselves to new levels of integrity, so that their relationships' integrity can grow as a result.

Wrapping Up

In this chapter, we've talked about the two different types of alignment that go into a person's integrity: *internal* alignment, or a clear sense of who you are; and *external* alignment, which is a pattern of living authentically with what you believe. We've also explored how in order for a relationship to have the integrity to survive the timelines that other people try to thrust on it, both individuals need to have enough integrity (internal and external alignment) so that the two of them can stand up together and say, "This is who we are; take us or leave us."

As the Couples by Intention couples and I begin to see the end of the course coming, the ability to stand with integrity and face the world becomes very important, since the group is about to come to a close. We'll explore these ideas further in Chapter 9, but first, it's time to reflect on what you'll take from Chapter 8.

Journal Questions

Chapter 8 Reflections

Now that you've reached the end of Chapter 8, it's time to reflect on what you've learned. Grab your journal and spend some time responding to these questions. After reading Chapter 8:

1. What will you *keep doing* in your life and relationship that you are already doing?

2. What will you *start* doing, based on what you learned?

3. What will you *stop* doing?

4. What will you *think more about*?

Maintaining the Plateau— Lasting for the Long Haul

In this chapter, you will:

- Learn what it means to live in a "plateau" moment in your relationship

- Listen to group members encouraging each other as they get close to finishing the Couples by Intention season

- Discuss the reality that it's normal for couples to be working on different aspects of their relationship at varying paces all at once

At some point in the Couples by Intention process—usually around week ten—it's inevitable that we begin talking about what will happen after the group stops meeting on a weekly basis. These amazing people, as they come to the end of a period of tremendous growth and development as individuals and as couples, begin to feel the weight of their work. A common reaction to the end of the group is pure ambivalence: they're ready for a break, but they don't want the work to end!

At this point in the group's journey, we begin to talk about the issue of relationship maintenance and plateaus. The core questions at this stage include: "When do you know that your relationship has hit a plateau?" and, "Is it okay that when it hits a plateau, you are in maintenance mode?" and, "What if we find that only one of us hits a plateau? Does it mean that we're not working, not being intentional, or losing our curiosity?"

▼

The growth in a relationship is not a steady climb; it comes in fits and starts.

▲

The growth in a relationship is not a steady climb; it comes in fits and starts. I explain to the group that the work looks like a recording studio. The relationship itself is the sound that is being made, the beautiful music of the individual singer or the duo singing in harmony. The work and growth in the relationship is the modulation that is being done at the mixing board. In a studio, the mixing board is a control panel with lots of dials and slide levels that help the artists to modulate the sounds and tones, helping the tracks to sound exactly as the musicians want them to. Sometimes, mixing involves working on the vocals; at other times, mixing focuses on the instrumentation, or on adding in a special track that was recorded outside of the session.

Relationships work like that studio. At any given time, we might be working on certain specific issues, while other issues have hit a plateau and are just "maintaining" in the background. We know they're there; we'll focus on them when we have the time, energy, and need. But we allow them to lie still for a time, so that we can focus on the areas we've agreed to improve.

Couples collectively and individually work on many aspects of their unions at the same time, perhaps focusing on improving communication, growing in intimacy, developing career plans, or deciding if they want a child. Each of these life experiences (along with many others) has its own journey and requires its own focus. For example, at one point when you met them, Sam and Yolanda were working together on their concerns and challenges with fertility. Ethan was working on his "presentation" as a transgender male, sharing his new self-understanding with Valerie as he discovered new, deeper layers of himself. John was trying to understand and work on his lack of career ambition. As he better understood that and grew in this area, he brought it to Meili, and they worked collaboratively together to craft how his workplace and career fit into their relationship.

If you look at each couple's relationship that way, it meant that each couple was necessarily always on a plateau (resting spot) for some area of work in their relationship while actively and intentionally working on other aspects of themselves and their connectedness with each other. Being on a plateau and in maintenance mode in some area of a relationship doesn't mean that we forget about it or neglect it. Just the opposite: maintenance is active, not passive. It involves holding something in place with the same intentionality and curiosity that got it to the plateau in the first place, even though neither partner is looking to stretch it further at that particular time. It's important to ensure that we don't let it diminish again due to default. Inevitably, because it's only possible to manage so many things at a time and our focus is limited, there are items that will begin to slip into old patterns. That's natural. The question, though, is how much we allow our work to slip before we decide that it's important enough to go back and work on it again. These things have to be decided together as a couple.

The reality of having to exist and work on so many levels at the same time can be quite challenging. Partners have to know which areas they're working on, and which things they're maintaining on a plateau, in order just to have enough curiosity to connect with their beloved in the areas they *are* working on. What makes a multiple approach like this one even more challenging is that one partner may be working in one area while the other partner is focusing on another—and they're both working together in a third area. One partner, for example, may be focusing their personal work on communicating better, while the other partner may be working on managing personal finances, and together they're working on creating and maintaining sacred space. (See Figure 11 for an image of what these dynamics can look like in a relationship.)

As the group comes to understand the multiple playing fields, their comments and reactions become even more animated. A session toward the end of a group's time together usually starts with a focus on what challenges the couples are facing as they work to

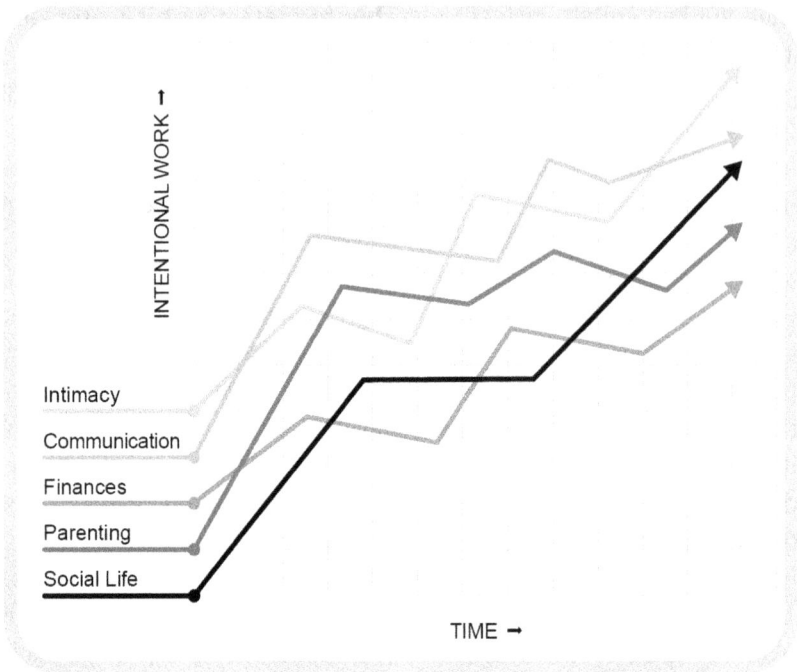

Figure 12: Typical Growth Patterns in an Intentional Relationship

maintain the growth and feel good about the plateau phases after a period of investment. Here's an example of one such exchange.

Bradley: Kids! [*Laughter from the group*] No, really. Kids, they are the biggest challenges. It seems that every time I think I have parented and got the kids to a great place so that I can focus on something else, they change and require my attention again. You can never take a break when you have kids. It is the one area where you never get to take my focus away.

Meili: I am at worst in the plateau stages. I am at my best in crisis and challenge. The plateau feels so uncomfortable for me that I will often create a crisis or challenge so that I can feel better, be on my game. Peaceful is hard for me. It doesn't feel **natural.**

John: [To Meili.] That is so true! That is exactly what happens.

[To the group.] What does maintenance look like? I don't even know. It never feels like we get there. We never get to take our guard down, so I'm not sure I would even be able to identify a plateau.

Mark: I get comfortable and confident, and then I do things that bring me back and trigger challenging behaviors. It puts me right back into work mode. So I guess I get a plateau, but I don't notice when it starts, and when I feel it, it doesn't last long. What I am learning is that I have to be more intentional about naming the plateau, and remember that a plateau doesn't mean ignoring the work and growth we did. It just means that we aren't working that hard in that area right now. We are focused somewhere else for a while. But I can't just ignore what we did.

Emilio: I need constant progress. I don't need the chaos or the crisis. I don't want that! But I need to be always moving forward. If it feels like we aren't working, I feel like we are falling. So, for me, I think when we are working hard is the plateau. That's when I'm the most comfortable and I'm feeling like things are stable and level. I don't like to run the risk of being lazy.

Mark: See, he's always in a "Go, go, go!" mode. That is hard for me. I have ADD and sometimes my focus just isn't there, and it makes him crazy. For me, I guess the plateau is when I feel comfortable and we are in a rhythm. But what makes us comfortable is not the same. When I am too comfortable, I get stalled out and lose my mojo. So, knowing that being in a maintenance mode means you still have to be intentional and curious—Wait, hold on . . . This is all making sense. Emilio, do you think that when I hit a plateau I'm no longer working or curious or intentional?

Emilio: That is my fear. It's like I and our relationship start to lose your focus, so I'm always pushing so we don't get lazy. I care about this relationship so much, but I don't like it when it feels lazy.

Mark: Hold on, hold on, hold on . . . I need to pull this all together. So, there are times you think I'm not choosing you and the relationship because I'm not actively letting you know that.

Emilio: Yes.

Mark: Wow. I have some work to do. I am going to think a lot more about maintenance, and how important it is that I don't lose my mojo—and make you feel like I am not here and in it with you.

As the group continues to process the dynamic of intentionally working on some aspect of relationship while allowing other aspects to be in an active maintenance plateau, they began to discuss how they manage working in different ways at the same time. The insights were as diverse as the group itself; everyone had a different approach.

Yolanda: We're just constantly talking, so it all gets jumbled together. It all just feels like a "we."

Sam: [To Yolanda.] What I learned is that some of it has to be a "me" and it is up to me to let you know when that is the case, because it isn't always a "we."

Yolanda: That's fair. I am curious to know what that is. We have to talk about that.

Bradley: Talking is such a foreign concept to me. I never felt a plateau until about four weeks ago when I finally was able to say some things that I have been holding for a really long time. It was hard, but we were able to have some real shared understanding. It's fucking fantastic! So I guess I'm experiencing a bit of my first plateau now. I'll let you all know how it goes! I don't know how long it will last, but for the first time in our relationship I feel like we are in that maintenance mode that you have all been talking about. I never felt it before. I am not ignoring it, but it feels great not to have to feel like I am stretching and exerting so hard all the time.

Carol: And that is a challenge for me. I have always wanted to create a space where we can talk and connect. What I have learned is that if I can slow down—ask myself, "What does this mean to Bradley?" and just be—I don't have to fix it. I don't have to manage it. I don't have to control it. What I have come to realize is that when I can focus on what Bradley does give me and look at it as a gift, I can appreciate him more and I will get more from him.

Elliott: Bradley, what does that mean to you that Carol realizes that what you give her is a gift?

Bradley: [Visibly moved.] I am amazed. I think that is all I ever really wanted.

Elliott: I am glad you are getting what you wanted. But, can you talk about what that means to you?

Bradley: Hmmm . . . It means that it is actually a gift I give myself. I am learning that when I open myself up and share with Carol, I can be validated. I always expected to be validated from the outside, but what it means to me is that I have to put something out there in order to be validated. Carol has to have something to respond to. In some ways that scares me. We made this big leap in our relationship and are on this plateau that I am loving and I am waiting for the other shoe to drop. If it does, then I am going to have to figure out how to get back. It scares me.

Carol: [to Bradley] Do you expect perfect every day? I think you expect it to be perfect every day.

Bradley: No. I don't expect perfect. I just hope for no craziness. It's the chaos that shuts me down.

Carol: I know there was a time where I wasn't able to help because of my own challenges. Now I'm helping more. I just want to be sure that maintenance doesn't mean perfect. Maintenance means it's okay for now. Is that a plateau? Things aren't always going to be the same. But what you see and think is stable and what I see and think is stable is different. I can only do me. I worry that sometimes your standards are too high and are unable to be met.

Bradley: I agree. I have to learn to talk to you about that. I have some work to do here. Maybe the next thing I have to work on is understanding my standards.

This exchange really showed the group the difference between work that's shared between the partners and work that is individual. Sam and Yolanda are always talking; they will continue to work on the "me versus we." Bradley and Carol need to continue growing this new communication skill that was so transformative for Bradley. For that to happen, Bradley has some additional individual work to do so that he can better understand his standards and his ability to articulate his thoughts, feelings, and understandings to Carol.

I challenge the group to think through how they will hold on to curiosity, intention, and loving relationship when everything is operating at different levels collectively and individually. The group developed an overall agreement that it was critical to continue talking about the relationship and how they were connecting beyond life tasks and responsibilities. They wanted to get to the deeper meaning and to ensure it was safe for each partner to be heard.

Ethan and Valerie described a significant area of growth, one that has allowed them to begin new areas of intentional work in the days since they finished Couples by Intention.

Ethan: [To Valerie.] In the beginning, I was so avoidant because of your internal processing about how you were afraid of what I would think and do. I just couldn't go there.

Valerie: I know. [Turning to me.] He asks. All the time. Questions! What happens now is that he opens me up. It's comforting. I feel that he cares and that I'm not a burden. He isn't asking me what's wrong or the types of questions that made me cautious. He asks me what my experience is. It's so much more meaningful. And then, I can start to think that he has lived through some shit too. Why is my shit harder or more challenging than his? It isn't the same, but when I can sit back and realize that we both have our histories and our strengths, I don't have to protect him from me. I have really learned that I was "helping" him and that I needed to stop. It wasn't my place. When I let him do his work, I get back so much more!

One of the important concepts that the group begins to grasp toward the end of the Couples by Intention season is that being able to operate on different levels requires the ability to create and hold space for each other. It's a concept that most of the participants had never experienced before coming to therapy. I talk about the importance of this skill early in my connections with my clients, but it becomes significantly more meaningful through the work of the group.

Creating and holding space is the act of cultivating an atmosphere that feels safe and secure, allowing individuals to have their reactions and explorations without interference, critique, "helping," or judgment. Members can ask questions, give support, share confirmations of understanding, and reinforce confidentiality. It is critical that we actively avoid interactions that interfere with the work. In the beginning of couple's therapy and in the first session or two of the group, I spend a great deal of energy enforcing the creation of space, so that everyone in the room is able to work at their own pace on the concerns that matter to them, gleaning their own learning along the way. Because everyone works at their own pace, it becomes critical that we don't push, prod, or drag someone else along. That's another version of the No-Helping Rule. If we are supportive, but not helping, each individual will be able to have their own self-discovery.

Journal Questions

Plateaus and Maintenance

Plateaus and active maintenance are the areas in a relationship where you have done a significant body of work and are ready to focus elsewhere. Pause here for a few minutes and write in your journal in response to these questions:

1. How would you know that you have completed a body of work? What indicators would you have that you are on a plateau?

2. Maintenance is an active stage. How do you remain intentional and curious while you are not working at a high level on a particular aspect of your relationship?

3. Work can be a shared or individual activity. What do you need so that you can work in both ways?

Wrapping Up

In this final chapter, we've discussed what it's like to come to a "plateau" in your relationship, and we've looked at the ways in which couples grow at different paces in different areas of their connection, all at the same time. It's around this time that the Couples by Intention group is getting ready to move on to the next phase of their lives, carrying what they learned in their three months together in group therapy forward into their day-to-day experience.

How will you take what *you've* learned in Chapter 9 forward into your own practices and the way you relate to your significant other? Take a moment to reflect one final time on what you've learned in the chapter.

Journal Questions

Chapter 9 Reflections

In your journal, respond to these questions. After reading Chapter 9:

1. What will you *keep doing* in your life and relationship that you are already doing?
2. What will you *start* doing, based on what you learned?
3. What will you *stop* doing?
4. What will you *think more about*?

Epilogue: A Letter from a Client

I have learned so much by sitting in my office chair and listening to my clients—really listening, with as much curiosity as I can muster, just like I invite them to do. Being intentional about one's relationship isn't rocket science, but that doesn't mean it's easy. To be intentional, both partners have to be intentional *individually*, understanding their choices and making decisions so that they can approach their partner ready to work together. In order to operate with this level of intention, each person must be awake and present, showing up for themselves and for their relationships.

As you look at your own life and relationships, challenge the notion and the expectations that relationships are supposed to be self-managing and just take care of themselves. That's television. You live in real life. Defy the inclination to have a relationship "by default," one that runs on autopilot. Relationships that work well are those in which the partners are working the relationship consistently. Being intentional requires that one think about what is happening and make clear decisions about how to move forward, sharing that process with one's partner along the way.

Having a clear focus on learning how to proceed and what the goals are is the first step. This is an intimate journey that you and your partner are taking together. Remember that intimacy is a balance of safety and vulnerability, and that achieving that balance requires intentional curiosity about yourself and about your partner. To develop that kind of curiosity, you'll need to create a language of intimacy, which is what we've been doing throughout this book. Think about how you talk about your body, your desires, your dreams—and learn to express them with your partner in a way that allows intentional curiosity to grow. In short: be curious about your partner, and learn not to know everything.

An intentional connection isn't about being "right." As we saw in this book, it's possible both to be right and to lose at the same time. Rather, connection is about *winning*—winning at a goal that is mutually defined and mutually beneficial. Curiosity and the freedom not to know carry the added benefit of creating a space that allows both partners to show up, bringing different stories and knowledge to how you relate to each other. Doing this can make for a richer, fuller experience and allow you to have a relationship with the person who is in front of you *now*, at *this* moment—not the person you met years ago, or the person you idealize them to be, or the person you hope they will grow into. Who is the person in front of you *today*? What are *this* person's quirks, stories, fascinations, flaws, beauties, messes, turn-ons, likes, loves? What makes *this* person tick?

Only when each partner allows themselves to encounter the other person as they *really* are can there be a "couple" at all—and only then can the couple come together to figure out what a winning connection would look like for them. These are crafted together, adjusted over time, and won by swagger—the ability to acknowledge your partner's experience and presence intentionally.

Being an intentional couple is rooted in choosing each other daily. You have to make a choice every day: stay, or go? Know why you are making that choice today—just today, that's all—and then be curious about what can happen next. That's how the best relationships grow and deepen over time.

As we've seen in this book, each person has to continue to explore who they are as unique people (internal alignment) and how they will bring their authentic selves to their relationship, while also holding the relationship in the world (external alignment). That's no easy task, and individuals have to be able to struggle through their own growth (the No-Helping Rule). Learn to create and hold space for each other as each partner does their own heavy lifting. Develop sacred space so that there is something special that can cement you together as you do the work of becoming more authentic.

Couples also have to learn to communicate with richness. Speak from the "I" statement, and listen with intentional curiosity (bearing witness and expanding the story). Take in the stories and experiences of your partner, because doing so can ground us in connection together as couples.

Be sure to acknowledge when you are finished with a body

of work, and take the opportunity to shift your active intention to another area. Being successful in the maintenance mode is an active process. Be sure to hold onto the work you have done and not lose it!

After the Couples by Intention group has finished its twelve weeks together, the couples in the group tend to stay connected and begin a mutual supportive social connection on their own (though you'll remember from Chapter 1 that this is never required). After sharing so much, it's natural to have a desire to build on the intimacy they have developed. I am often invited to group members' socials, potlucks, and family events. But I make it a point to step out of the group when the group process is complete, because I want to make sure not to interfere with the group members' progress by staying unhelpfully involved in their lives after our time together. They have to learn to fly. Some couples will continue to do couple's work with me outside of the group because they want to deepen their skills or they feel that they are not yet complete with the change they want to see, and I'll often work with them for a time longer. But for the couples that don't continue therapy outside the group, I don't always get to know what happens next.

Every once in a while, though, I get a surprise message.

A Letter From Carol

About a year and half after Bradley and Carol finished their time in Couples by Intention, I got a long email from Carol. She told me how hard the past months had been as she and Bradley tried to implement all they had learned. She spoke of having difficult conversations and of feeling discomfort when they intentionally stopped retreating and faced their challenges. She described the hard work of resetting boundaries with their children to create more space for their marriage, and of the joy of finding the courage to be sexy again. And perhaps most importantly, she talked about how she and Bradley realized that they needed to forgive each other and themselves for all the struggles and incompetencies they had brought to their marriage.

One night, she wrote, they had been lying in bed after sex, and they found themselves laughing because they had had sex without a huge emotional struggle to get there. "Sex just happened," she beamed. "We were just there in the bedroom and we had sex. We didn't think about it—we just did it! And it was good!"

This was the moment that Carol and Bradley had talked about wanting when they first met me: to have sex and intimacy and feel normal while doing it. But there was more. Attached to the email was a picture. It was of Carol in her wedding dress and Bradley in a suit. "We get a babysitter every month now," she wrote, "someone to take the kids out of the house. Then we put on our wedding clothes and recommit to each other. As it turns out, we never forgot how to say, 'I choose you.'"

I can only marvel at what Carol and Bradley, and so many other couples, have done, and go back one more time to what my Grandma Annie told me: "Do your work now or do your work later—but everyone has to do their work." Some things, as it turns out, never change.

About the Author

ELLIOTT KRONENFELD, Ph.D. LICSW, CSTS is a certified sex therapist who works with individuals and couples to find greater meaning in their connections. As the owner and founder of Insight Psychotherapy in the Boston area, Elliott specializes in helping couples work through intimacy, infertility, and infidelity challenges. He lives near Boston with his partner and children.

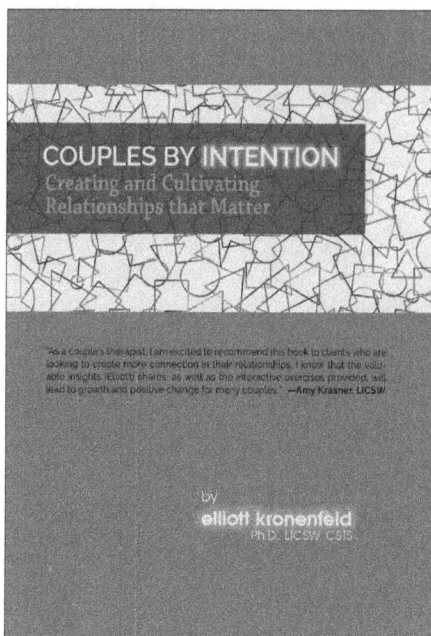

Couples by Intention

Creating and Cultivating Relationships that Matter

Elliott Kronenfeld, Ph.D. LICSW, CSTS

www.couplesbyintention.com

Publisher: SDP Publishing
Also available in ebook format

TO PURCHASE:

SDP Publishing.com
Barnes & Noble.com
Amazon.com

Available at all major bookstores

SDP Publishing

www.SDPPublishing.com
Contact us at: info@SDPPublishing.com